Scan QR code to learn
about the companion course!

THEBELONGING.CO

The Path of Presence
The Belonging Co

Copyright © 2014-2024

The Belonging Co all rights reserved. No part of this publication may be reproduced, stored in a retrieval system or transmitted in any form or by any means, electronic, mechanical, recording or otherwise without the prior permission of the publisher or in accordance with the previous of the Copyright, Designs and Patents Act 1988 or under the terms of any license permitting limited copying issued by the Copyright Licensing Agency.

Scripture References:
All Scripture quotations are from the ESV Bible (The Holy Bible, English Standard Version)

Published by:
The Belonging Co
201 Great Circle Rd.
Nashville, TN 37228

Editors:
Kylie Rasmussen
Amber Essman
Sarah Squires

Special thanks to One Hope for contributing to this publication.

Printed in USA

THE PATH OF PRESENCE

A Discipleship of Dwelling with Jesus

Written by Paul Bergin

THE BELONGING Co

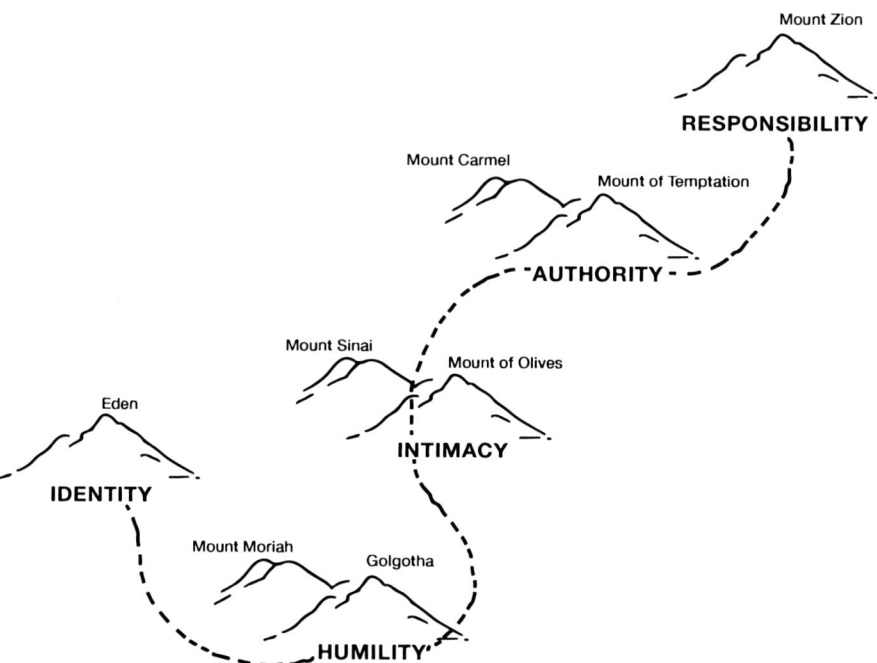

PREFACE 6

IDENTITY
The Mountain of Eden 10

HUMILITY
Mount Moriah to Mount Golgotha 38

INTIMACY
Mount Sinai to the Mount of Olives 67

AUTHORITY
Mount Carmel to the Mount of Temptation 110

RESPONSIBILITY
Mount Zion 142

PREFACE

If you have been following Jesus for any length of time, you have probably heard the word "discipleship." Discipleship and following Jesus are in essence the same thing, although in our modern context we sometimes make discipleship a formal checklist of sorts with things like Bible reading, prayer, and church attendance on it. The reality of following Jesus as Lord, as an organic, relational, presence-filled friendship can be rare for humans and even Christians. Specific practices like prayer and Bible reading are vital tools in our discipleship to Jesus, but ritualistic performance of these things can leave us unchanged and desirous for an authentic intimacy. Many of us are still asking questions like: Who am I? What am I supposed to be doing with my life? Where is God? Why can't I sense him?

How can we understand what true discipleship to Jesus is? Well, when we first believe, our spirits are awakened to faith by the power of the Holy Spirit and from there our hearts begin to long for true transformation, purpose beyond programming, and a deepening of our relationship with God. It's a soul-call to the soul-creator and only in the presence of God will we find the answers to these questions and this yearning. The presence of God is where true discipleship takes place.

When you are looking to start something, you want to begin with the end in mind. Discipleship is no exception. Where do you want to end up? Or a better question, with whom do you want to end up? Well, to the second question, hopefully the true Jesus who is God, is the one you really want to end up with. The first question of our ultimate end is laid out for us in the final book of the canon of Scripture, Revelation:

"And I heard a loud voice from the throne saying, 'Behold, the dwelling place of God is with man. He will dwell with them, and they will be his people, and God himself will be with them as their God.'" (Revelation 21:3 ESV)

In the church, we often talk about humanity being created for a relationship with God. Here we see that is exactly where God intends for us to end up — with him! If we read further in this passage, we see that this destination is not just a location, but God's very presence, alive and engaged.

"And I saw no temple in the city, for its temple is the Lord God the Almighty and the Lamb. And the city has no need of sun or moon to shine on it, for the glory of God gives it light, and its lamp is the Lamb." (Revelation 21:22–23)

This is the atmosphere of wonder and glory we long for. Our internal, spiritual wiring for this eternity calls to us. The comforting thing for us living our daily life on this broken planet is that this is not just a future final dwelling place, but something we get to experience — because of Jesus — in the here and now as we follow him, living our life as his disciples.

If that's true, what does it look like to dwell with God? How do we do that? What does this kind of discipleship to Jesus look like? What does it mean for me in my walk with God? These are some of the questions this book aims to address.

If you are looking for a "How To" guidebook on specific spiritual disciplines, this is not that. There are many incredible books out there on discipleship tools though. This book, however, while touching on some of those things, will adjust the lens of how we view our discipleship to Jesus and how we are changed in the presence of God. This is a journey through the text of the Bible from Genesis to Revelation focused on the transformative presence of God. Life is a journey and we are given the opportunity to choose what kind of path we will follow, how we live our life. We can choose the path of God's presence.

Along this path of his presence, we will use points of encounter in the story of the Bible where God's presence came down to the earth and revealed parts of his character, intention, and plan for us. Each of these points of encounter was marked on a mountain with a patriarch or leader of Israel, God's people in the Old Testament narrative. These revealed aspects of God's presence build upon each other, deepening our discipleship to Jesus.

Before we begin the journey along the path of presence, we have to establish first: what is the presence of God? The ultimate revelation of God is found in the person of Jesus. God becoming flesh here on earth demonstrates his desire for us to experience his presence. His presence is evidenced on the earth through his birth, death, and resurrection and then testified by miracles, signs and wonders, an internal sense of nearness and peace, the persuasion to faith, and even creation itself — all promised outworkings of the Kingdom of God operating on Earth. God's presence, however, is not limited to things we see or feel. God's presence, in the way we are going to be talking about, is the continuous, conscious awareness of his nearness and involvement in every area of our life ongoing. As disciples, we want to recognize it at all moments in all situations. Yet the reality of his presence is not activated by our awareness; more, that his presence activates our awareness of his reality.

This is an invitation to be discipled and transformed in the ways of Jesus through living and dwelling in the presence of God. In the presence of God, we are about to discover our established <u>identity</u>, the power of an attitude of <u>humility</u>, a sense of true <u>intimacy</u>, our Spirit-empowered <u>authority</u>, and a call toward our God-designed <u>responsibility</u> on this earth. Come, enter the path of his presence.

IDENTITY

The Mountain of Eden

*Encountering who God our Father is
so that we might know who we are
and live accordingly.*

Have you ever ventured on a hike, or even a walk around your neighborhood, thinking it would be one thing but it ends up being another? Maybe it rains halfway through. Maybe it's a steeper climb than your smartphone suggested. Maybe there are exposed roots or cracks in the sidewalk that cause you to lose your footing. Maybe you wind up down a street you hadn't meant to because you were lost in thought. When we start a journey — whether an arduous hike or a turn around your cul-de-sac — we can have a goal or destination, but we will always be surprised by new information along the path that we couldn't have anticipated when we left our front door.

When we put our faith in Jesus, our spirit is brought from death to life and an awareness of God awakens in us by the power of the Holy Spirit. From this point, we become not only aware of our sin and shortcomings, but of the goodness and grace of God. This awareness persuades us to faith and sparks a lifelong journey with God where we are continuously transformed and changed in his presence. This is true discipleship.

Unfortunately, we are initially blinded to the reality that there is a Creator, a Father, a God — the God that has created us for a specific purpose. So we follow our own desires and idols. We deify our own dreams and become our own gods. The Apostle Paul says this, summarizing truth in 2 Corinthians 4:4:

In their case the god of this world has blinded the minds of the unbelievers, to keep them from seeing the light of the gospel of the glory of Christ, who is the image of God.

To put it simply, we cannot see correctly. We cannot see the light, the glory, JESUS — who is our creator God because Satan has blinded us. We need help!

Whether you are at the beginning of your journey with Jesus or have been following him for decades, you have experienced the presence of God. To walk this path called life with an awareness of the presence of God — his nearness, his accessibility, his involvement, his goodness, his sovereignty — is to walk the path of presence. There are many paths to choose from in this life, but only the path of his presence offers the transformation, friendship, guidance, joy, and security Jesus promises to those following him.

One of the foundational parts of discipleship to Jesus is a rediscovery of our identity. We need to understand from what and from whom we draw our identity in order to move forward on the path of presence. We have a creator who created us for relationship with him. We also have an enemy who hates us and wants us anywhere but the path of presence. He wants to steal your confidence, kill your sense of God's nearness, and destroy your renewal in Jesus Christ. His power is limited, his antics predictable, but his persistence strong. If we don't know who we are and the implications of that, we won't get far without being misled, distracted, or worst of all, give up in discouragement. Thankfully, God gave us a record of who we were created to be at the beginning of the Biblical narrative and from there we can begin to reestablish and remember who he is and who we are because of him.

The mountains covered in this book are recorded points of encounter where God's presence visibly entered the realm of Earth and revealed his character, power, and intention for humanity. We can learn so much about the presence of God by looking back to these moments of encounter.

In the Bible, mountains are places where God often encounters his people in an observable way — a Theophany, if you like. They were viewed as places where Earth meets Heaven. While God is omnipresent, meaning he can be everywhere at once, his presence is intentional and personal in revealing who he is at certain stages throughout the Old and New Testaments, often experienced as tangible intersections that connect Heaven's realities to Earth. Ancient cultures also believed that mountainous places were where the gods of the cosmos encountered mortals, yet they were places of only temporary dwelling. God's original story with mankind would end much differently. The God of Genesis chose a garden called "Paradise" within a mountain, a place to walk with mankind, to be with mankind, and to allow mankind to expand it.

THE MOUNTAIN OF EDEN

The first point of encounter with the presence of God for humanity was at the beginning in Eden — meaning "paradise."

A river flowed out of Eden to water the garden, and there it divided and became four rivers. (Genesis 2:10)

Eden can be identified as an elevated place in which water could flow from to the garden. Its one entrance that was eventually guarded (Gen 3:24) might also allude to the steepness of its access. While Genesis doesn't outrightly state its raised position, the book of Ezekiel gives us insight into Eden imagery in what he describes as the mountain of God and at the same time the garden of God (Ezekiel 28:13-16).

The LORD God took the man and put him in the garden of Eden to work it and keep it. (Genesis 2:15 ESV)

Eden is believed to be a place of incredible beauty. God calls it good! Within this mountain there was a garden, not like your backyard variety, but more like the beauty of a wild forest. If we were to use word association, when we hear "the Garden of Eden," our first thoughts typically identify it as the place where Adam and Eve succumbed to the serpent's temptation and the consequence of their disobedience was rendered. We think of the moment when the image of God in man was distorted through the deception of Satan. A common starting point when discussing discipleship is this very thing: sin. However, the actual place of Eden is often overlooked. To jump straight to the sin problem and overlook Eden — the platform of this relational story unfolding — is to miss something of the nature and image of God, and therefore, to miss something of ourselves. It is to miss the real beginning of the story.

OUR IDENTITY FOUND IN WALKING AND DWELLING WITH GOD

Ponder this: God, from the beginning, walked with humanity in a garden. Not in a city or on a street or in a library. He chose to walk with humanity amongst the elements of the earth – its soil, plants, and animals.

As noted, the Old Testament prophet Ezekiel referred to Eden as the *"garden of God, a Field with every precious stone... the holy mountain of God" (Ezekiel 28:13–16).* The Garden set in the east of Eden is somewhat interesting in that it is barren before it is beautiful.

When no bush of the field was yet in the land and no small plant of the field had yet sprung up—for the LORD God had not caused it to rain on the land, and there was no man to work the ground, and a mist was going up from the land and was watering the whole face of the ground—then the LORD God formed the man of dust from the ground and breathed into his nostrils the breath of life, and the man became a living creature. And the LORD God planted a garden in Eden, in the east, and there he put the man whom he had formed. And out of the ground the LORD God made to spring up every tree that is pleasant to the sight and good for food. The tree of life was in the midst of the garden, and the tree of the knowledge of good and evil. (Genesis 2:5–9)

The Garden doesn't grow before man is there to tend to it. God waits before he creates Adam so that the Garden can be sustained and expanded. God is not just interested in creating things, he is interested in dwelling with the people he created. From the beginning, God chooses to express his beauty and glory in and through mankind. We are the only creation made in his image.

God's relational, abiding, creative nature signals our identity as relational, abiding, creative beings.

God walks with Adam and Eve in the Garden.

And they heard the sound of the LORD God walking in the garden in the cool of the day, and the man and his wife hid themselves from the presence of the LORD God among the trees of the garden. But the LORD God called to the man and said to him, "Where are you?" And he said, "I heard the sound of you in the garden, and I was afraid, because I was naked, and I hid myself." (Genesis 3:8–10)

Yes, that's right. The God who created the Heavens and the Earth and everything in it — the all-knowing, all-seeing, never changing, ever-present, and sovereign God — walks with humans. His presence was there among the trees, talking and calling to Adam and Eve. Therefore, he cannot be reduced to an immaterial wind or force. This is an insightful revelation. God is showing himself to be personal. Walking with someone speaks of a journey, direction, or companionship, but it also implies to follow in a manner of life (Psalm 1:1, Psalm 15:3). God walks Adam's way, and Adam is to follow. God is Creator, yet his walking speaks of his friendship and his dwelling. He is their security, assurance, and provision, and the good news is he has never stopped desiring to walk with men and women — his children.

OUR IDENTITY FOUND IN THE CHARACTER OF GOD

To begin to rediscover our own identity, we know now that by spending time with our Creator, we can uncover parts of ourselves distorted by sin. We also begin to establish our identity by looking at the character of that Creator. Without providing an exhaustive list, here are some attributes the Bible describes about the walking, talking, personal God:

God is all powerful (Omnipotent): Is anything too hard for the Lord? (Genesis 18:14)

God is all knowing (Omniscient): For whenever our heart condemns us, God is greater than our heart, and he knows everything. (1 John 3:20)

God is infinite and beyond our notion of space (Omnipresent): And he is before all things, and in him all things hold together. (Colossians 1:17)

God's nature never changes (Immutable): God is not man, that he should lie, or a son of man, that he should change his mind. Has he said, and will he not do it? Or has he spoken, and will he not fulfill it? (Numbers 23:19)

God is Sovereign. He knows all purpose and design and outcomes: Remember the former things of old, for I am God, and there is no other; I am God, and there is none like me, declaring the end from the beginning and from ancient times things not yet done. (Isaiah 46:9–10)

God is one being, and he is three persons, who each share the same nature and essence: God is not divided into three parts, but his divinity is fully and wholly possessed by all three. Each person is equally God. (Galatians 4:6–7)

The greatest attribute of God is that he is holy. His nature is like no other and is often defined by what it is not, in comparison to everything else. It is undefiled, pure, glorious, and defined by the words that heavenly hosts sing over and over regarding God: holy.

And one called to another and said:
  "Holy, holy, holy is the LORD of hosts;
  the whole earth is full of his glory!" (Isaiah 6:3)

If you were to stop there, it would be enough for any human to marvel at. Yet perhaps the greatest mystery of all is that God, in his perfect holiness, chose to dwell with man. It is here we learn something profound about the identity of God: his immanence. His immanence tells us of his willingness and passionate desire to be intimately involved with his creation. This is perhaps the greatest mystery and a distinctly unique dimension of God. We begin to witness God as deeply personal. He is known as Father, not only to the Son but to us. He has children — billions of them — and he knows each by name and he places them with precision on this Earth and within the timeline of history purposefully. Ephesians 4:6 says, he is one God and Father of all, who is over all and through all and in all.

Contrasting the walking and dwelling of God our Father, is the counterfeit power of the gods of this world or the cosmos that we read about throughout history. They don't walk with humans. They dictate, demand, and spread fear for respect but they don't walk. No other god is seen communing with "mere mortals." Yet the true God dwells right in the midst of his creation. Only a relational God does that. Only a God who is a Father walks amongst his children and dwells with his creation. God walking with humanity speaks of his relational intent and his purpose for creation: to exist and live in his presence. He watches over creation. He provides, instructs, guides, and leads like the Father we desire.

Is not he your father, who created you, who made you and established you? (Deuteronomy 32:6)

As a father shows compassion to his children,
so the Lord shows compassion to those who fear him.
(Psalm 103:13)

But now, O LORD, you are our Father; we are the clay, and you are our potter; we are all the work of your hand. (Isaiah 64:8)

The challenge for us all is that our earthly fathers or parents don't always display the character and attributes of God the Father. Sin distorted and disrupted all relationships, not just the relationship between us and God, but person to person as well. "How can God be good if my own father is or was like [fill the blank]?" "How can

I trust him when I see so much pain and suffering in the world?" "If God is truly in the world, wouldn't he fix it?" "If he was deeply personal and walking with us, why is there so much pain, violence, sickness, and despair?" These are all relevant and common questions. As you read on, we will explore how God is more deeply acquainted with these questions than we know.

Millions of people existing today have consciously experienced (or subconsciously suppressed) anger, fear, disillusionment, or unbelief with God. God the Father has often not been displayed, taught, or modeled like the Father in which the Bible presents. Therefore, many are distant, pondering, or aimlessly naïve to the reality that God can be personal, that he cares, that he sees and knows, and that we can know something of God, the supreme Father of love.

All sin finds a common denominator in ultimately failing to trust God's character and follow his loving commands—that he is who he say he is, and that his way is the best.

OUR IDENTITY FOUND IN THE FAMILY OF GOD

It could be argued that the greatest problem in the world is not a poverty problem, a violence problem, a political problem, or a resource problem. The greatest issue the world has is an orphan problem. Not biological orphans — although this is a sobering reality. We are talking about an even deeper reality: spiritual sons and daughters who do not know their true Father and who are unaware that they are made in his image. Spiritual orphans are unaware that they are sustained by his Spirit and placed on Earth for a greater purpose than what their culture or upbringing might have communicated. We all have been, at one time or another, orphans who have been disconnected from our home with the Father and instead have searched the streets of this world to find a place we can call home. This is what sin is and does. It disconnects us from God our Father and orphans us.

Yes, God is in the world he created — as we will observe — but God is not of it. He stands outside, transcendent to time, matter, and space. He is not determined by his creation.

The Father we long for cannot be found in the home of the world but only in Spirit. He is reigning in a heavenly place beyond this Earth and yet over it, too. While Heaven is often spoken of as a place of eternity, it has also come to Earth bearing the Kingdom of God in the person of Jesus as we will explore. God is Spirit. Spirit, simply put, speaks of breath, even wind. It's the very essence of life apart from flesh. We cannot see the wind, but we definitely see its effects. Profoundly, God gives us a spirit distinct from animals so that we may engage with and come to know his Holy Spirit. It is the only reason we can know him as Father, crying "Abba" (Romans 8:16). *Abba* is an intimate Aramaic term that refers to the dependency and relationship of a child — a son and daughter.

For you did not receive the spirit of slavery to fall back into fear, but you have received the Spirit of adoption as sons, by whom we cry, "Abba! Father!" The Spirit himself bears witness with our spirit that we are children of God, and if children, then heirs — heirs of God and fellow heirs with Christ, provided we suffer with him in order that we may also be glorified with him. (Romans 8:15–17)

This is the identity we must see and come to learn to know in order to remove the tainted views of ourselves as orphans. We must explore the truth of the word of God for ourselves, allowing the Holy Spirit and also the relationship of others in community to help us see that we have a place in the family of God. Not just in a broad sense, but in a personal sense, God is your Father.

As the ultimate Father, we will observe that God uses words like "compassionate" and "gracious" and "merciful" to describe himself, and that is who he is, even in the midst of circumstances that don't appear good. We can be confident like the Psalmist, who says, "goodness and mercy shall follow me all the days of my life" (Psalm 23:6). As we follow Christ, who is the embodiment of goodness and mercy, we will know God as Father. We will be utterly assured of his presence that he is good, that he is intimate and that he is secure.

OUR IDENTITY FOUND IN THE MERCIFUL NATURE OF GOD

The Trinity is the most complex of relationships to understand. Perhaps we were never meant to fully know the workings of God in his Trinity while on earth. This is a mystery that requires all knowledge. This is why he is God and we are not. We only know in part, but one day we will know in full. All we have been given is all that we need to know for now. What we observe throughout the Bible are the functions and the personhood of The Father, Son, and Holy Spirit — especially when it comes to redeeming mankind.
Then God said, "Let us make man in our image, after our likeness." (Genesis 1:26a)

God desires relationship because he is relational. His very nature tells us this. God is triune, meaning three parts of one God, working together and serving one another in relationship with each other. God is one and intrinsically relational in nature. He is complete within himself. "The Trinity" is how we describe the threefold personhood of God. God in his supremacy is three persons in one. The Hebrew grammar depicts this in Genesis 1:26 in its usage of the word "us." It is in this image that we are created and called to reflect the attributes and relational nature of who he is. This leads us to the understanding that if God is holy and complete, relational, and self-sacrificing, our original identity and purpose is one of holiness, completeness, relationship, and to serve the world.

The implications of being made in God's image are essential for understanding who you are. So, why is it we often don't identify this way? Why does my identity feel untethered and up for debate? Why does my lived experience tell me something different?

Sin seems the obvious answer; missing the mark or separation from God's best is a simple definition, yet, the temptation to believe something else of the identity of God and therefore our identity is what undergirds our leading to sin. Look at the question Satan proposed to Adam and Eve in the garden about eating the fruit of the Tree of the Knowledge of Good and Evil that God said not to:

But the serpent said to the woman, "You will not surely die. For God knows that when you eat of it your eyes will be opened, and you will be like God, knowing good and evil." (Genesis 3:4–5)

All relational breakdown and distorted purposeful identity is witnessed through Satan's deception in Genesis, that we were not already "like God." That is, he led mankind to believe that we lacked something and that God was holding back something from us. The implications are that we search aimlessly in this world for an experience of intimacy that can only be reflected in the nature of God, and therefore our true image is left tainted, broken, and wavering without the revelation of who we truly are.

Here's the good news: despite our disobedience grounded in unbelief, God outlined his foreknowledge to send a savior, his Son, Jesus, to redeem us to our original image and place of dwelling with God. We have the opportunity to believe and be with him.

OUR IDENTITY FOUND IN GOD'S IMAGE

In Exodus 34, we see that God reveals his very nature and identity with a Hebrew man raised in the palaces of the Pharaohs of Egypt, called Moses. This is what the Father's presence is described like to him.

The LORD passed before him and proclaimed, "The LORD, the LORD, a God merciful and gracious, slow to anger, and abounding in steadfast love and faithfulness, keeping steadfast love for thousands, forgiving iniquity and transgression and sin, but who will by no means clear the guilty, visiting the iniquity of the fathers on the children and the children's children, to the third and the fourth generation." (Exodus 34:6-7)

When describing himself to Moses, mercy is the first attribute out of the mouth of God! Mercy in many ways, speaks of God withholding what we deserve and sustaining our life. He is a Father who gives and pursues love while we are still separate in our sin. He abounds in grace, giving us what we don't deserve. He forgives iniquity and transgressions.

He is very slow to anger — hundreds of years, slow. We see when his righteous anger is released upon Israel, many times he is handing them over to their own desires, reflecting his desire not to control humanity, but desiring a love response. The intent for Israel was for them to see the error of their ways and return to the loving mercy of God.

Jump centuries into the New Testament, and we see the first description of love in the Apostle Paul's writings, when he says, "love is patient" (1 Corinthians 13). God's presence is patient and kind. We recognize this from the way he dealt with Israel, time and time again. He forgave them for their worship of idols and other gods. He gave the Hebrew people the opportunity to have their sins and disobedience atoned for. He forgave Israel over hundreds and hundreds of years. And he is still the same God to those who turn to him today. He welcomes his children into his presence where there is repentance.

Mercy is required to know the presence of God; it should propel you towards him. Remember, he moved towards you first. Because of his mercy, we can rediscover our identity.

OUR IDENTITY IN THE PERSON OF JESUS

God is immanent — personal in the world — and the greatest evidence of this is Jesus. Jesus is God, he is God the Son, and he came to Earth.

And the Word became flesh and dwelt among us, and we have seen his glory, glory as of the only Son from the Father, full of grace and truth. (John 1:14)

The presence of God came dwelling in flesh, walking and talking with humanity just as God had done in some form, in the Garden of Eden with Adam and Eve. The path of presence has Jesus as the center of all civilization and the created cosmos because he has come down from God making the fullness of God visible. Jesus is God with us and he has made the Father's presence and plan known: to show the love and mercy of the Father.

In the beginning was the Word, and the Word was with God, and the Word was God. He was in the beginning with God. All things were made through him, and without him was not any thing made that was made. (John 1:1–3)

In Isaiah 7:14, it was prophesied that the virgin Mary shall conceive a child and call Him, "Immanuel," which means "God with us." Seven hundred years later, the Gospel of Matthew declares the reality and the awe and wonder of his presence with us:

All this took place to fulfill what the Lord had spoken by the prophet:

"Behold, the virgin shall conceive and bear a son,
and they shall call his name Immanuel"
(which means, God with us). (Matthew 1:22–23)

The majesty and mystery of God was made known. Immanuel was here — dwelling. Christ was present amongst his people in the union of two natures: one fully divine and the other fully human. God had graced the Earth he created. He stooped low to serve and save the lost. The personal God of Israel had been revealed as even more personal. The presence of the person of God — Jesus — walked alongside men, women, and children to love and guide and save the world.

For from his fullness we have all received, grace upon grace. For the law was given through Moses; grace and truth came through Jesus Christ. No one has ever seen God; the only God, who is at the Father's side, he has made him known. (John 1:16)

One greater than Moses had come — the new Moses, whose name means "drawn out of the water," or "delivered." Jesus would be the true Savior, the deliverer of a people drowning in their sin. Christ has made God the Father known.

Jesus is God — the eternal God, the one God, the incarnate Son of God — who came to reveal the unseen God. He was crucified, raised from the dead, and now dwells at the right hand of the Father. His presence is fully divine, perpetual, creative, and sustaining the life of all men and creation.

Our identity is therefore understood with the premise of not just what God says about himself, but also in what he does. Accepting the redemptive work of Jesus giving his life on the cross enables us to not only receive his salvation, but also conforms us to his image: merciful. In short, our identity is now full of hope, for today and for the future.

On our journey of discipleship to Jesus, knowing who he is actually helps us reconnect back to who we are. Our identity is uncovered in discovering the majesty and wonder of Jesus. So, what about Jesus should we focus on then? We are going to take a look in the remaining portion of this chapter at Jesus' grace, mercy, and transforming truth all found in his presence.

OUR IDENTITY FOUND IN THE GRACE OF JESUS

The people of Israel in the Old Testament viewed their walk with God as a gift of grace and mercy. Everything was given to them by God. The preservation of the oracles and words of God, the worship, the insight into his wisdom were all given by God. The glory of God was graciously given to Israel for the purpose of displaying God's nature and presence in the Earth, just like God's instructions were given to Adam and Eve.

They are Israelites, and to them belong the adoption, the glory, the covenants, the giving of the law, the worship, and the promises. To them belong the patriarchs, and from their race, according to the flesh, is the Christ, who is God over all, blessed forever. Amen. (Romans 9:4-5)

We may view the 613 laws given to Israel by God for them to obey, as laborious and burdensome. Israel viewed the giving of the law of God and to be a people who are set apart by him as a special honor, even despite how they wandered from God and disobeyed the law. What we may view as a binding and unnecessary law, they viewed as abundant grace. For through the law, the temporary atonement of their sins was made possible. Most of all, when the law was obeyed, the presence and blessing of God would remain with them.

Yet, Jesus came to fulfill the law, not abolish it (Matthew 5:17). The law was never evil. The Apostle Paul says it is good. At the same time, the law could never suffice for the salvation of mankind. It was a temporary guardian that only exposed our shortcomings and our need for a Savior (Galatians 3).

John says that "grace upon grace" was given. The first grace was given through the Old Covenant — the law of Moses. The second grace was given through the New Covenant in Jesus Christ, in whom all truth is found. It's the same grace, mercy, forgiveness, and the same righteousness that God revealed to Moses in Exodus 34. However, the New Covenant speaks of a greater grace that builds upon the former because it's a superior covenant. The New Covenant now enables Jew and Gentile (the nations) to experience this grace. Jesus Christ the Messiah died for our sin once and for all. Grace is now greater in its expression and reality because the Spirit of God has enabled us all access to the Father. It's no longer just one high priest who has access to the presence of God. We all — Jew and Gentile — have access to the throne room and the glorious presence of God. The New Covenant is also greater because the sting of death and the consequence of sin have been destroyed by Jesus Christ forever. Jesus died on the cross and overcame death by being raised to life again by the Father.

When God says he will punish the sins of those who disobey him to the third and fourth generation in Exodus 34, we can now rest assured: Jesus Christ took the punishment for our sins and carried the curse of every generational sin upon himself. His mercy also speaks of his justice and holy nature. The power of iniquity and transgression stops and is made "just" with the appropriation of blood and sacrifice of Jesus in our lives. We no longer have any need for animal sacrifice, as outlined in the law of Moses.

Just as Adam and Eve covered themselves with clothes that they made from fig leaves when they hid from God, which represented a temporary atonement, now, the presence of Jesus, his body, and his blood forgives our sin. Animal blood will not suffice.

In the Gospel of John, Jesus says the most amazing statement about himself to Thomas:

Jesus said to him, "I am the way, and the truth, and the life. No one comes to the Father except through me. If you had known me, you would have known my Father also. From now on you do know him and have seen him." (John 14:6–7)

Jesus is the map. He is the only right direction to the Father and the true adventure of the journey. If you want to walk in the presence and identity of your Father, you have to do it through Jesus Christ. The grace we experience in Jesus centers our whole identity around his goodness and sacrifice on our behalf. We are not out there on our own struggling to find our self, our purpose, our own absolvement. We are anchored in the grace of Christ. You don't need your own selfish plan, the plan of grace has been mapped out for you. The way we see this play out in our life is that when we acknowledge and follow the truth of his word, we are experiencing his grace and are communing with God at the same time, conforming to his pattern of life, his likeness, and his identity for us. When you know Christ as the center of your identity, you simultaneously know the Father and the Holy Spirit's plan for your life.

Your identity is not a better version of you. Remember, we are inherently sinful. Striving to become a better person will only lead to more versions of sin. We need to be reborn and renewed again. Only Jesus has the power to do that. Our own efforts will always fall short. You can lean on God's grace and mercy.

Jesus Christ has become our identity. Full stop.

OUR IDENTITY FOUND IN THE MERCY OF JESUS

If the grace of Jesus makes it possible for our identity to be realized in him, the mercy of Jesus absorbs our guilt, shame, and condemnation from sin and allows us to experience his life. The Apostle Paul carries the notion and reality of mercy into the New Testament in Ephesians 2:4–9:

But God, being rich in mercy, because of the great love with which he loved us, even when we were dead in our trespasses, made us alive together with Christ — by grace you have been saved — and raised us up with him and seated us with him in the heavenly places in Christ Jesus, so that in the coming ages he might show the immeasurable riches of his grace in kindness toward us in Christ Jesus. For by grace you have been saved through faith. And this is not your own doing; it is the gift of God, not a result of works, so that no one may boast.

The same mercy describing God's character in Exodus 34 is found in Christ's love and sacrifice for us. Our punishment for our sin was instead poured out on Christ, this is the immeasurable riches of grace and kindness. This is the best news you will ever hear! This is only an act of a personal God, who was so passionate to dwell with you forever. When you were dead in your sin, he made you alive in Christ (Ephesians 2:5).

> *Surely his salvation is near to those who fear him,*
>   *that glory may dwell in our land.*
> *Steadfast love and faithfulness meet;*
>   *righteousness and peace kiss each other. (Psalm 85:9–10)*

Steadfast mercy kissed righteousness and peace in the sacrifice of Jesus sent by the Father. The merciful sacrifice made it "just" for mankind to live free from sin and reunited with Father, that his glory could dwell in you.

What was the consequence when Eve disobeyed God? It was expulsion from the garden — a cutting off from the manifest presence of their Father. The dwelling stopped, the abiding was no more, and their security and peace had now been replaced by fear and lack. The mountain and garden of paradise, where the place of their identity and purpose had been given, has been affected by sin. By their own choice, they had made themselves orphans and enemies of God (Romans 5:10).

But God had made provision for humanity's sin before they had even disobeyed. Only a good Father sees the error of his children before they do it and acts in kindness. Although man's days would now be numbered and physical death would be made certain, the Father had redemption — of body, soul, and spirit — in mind. Because God is holy, excommunication for mankind from the garden was the only solution. God's presence in the garden meant unholiness and sin could have no remnant there.

Later on in Israel's journey, God would ask the Israelites to build an ark, a gold chest that represented the covenant God had made with his people. The golden ark would have a lid — *kaporet* in Hebrew, which can be translated "mercy seat," because it was the special place of his presence and atonement for Israel's sin. The garden was guarded with angels protecting re-entry with swords, and Cherubim angels were also on either side of the lid, protecting the presence of God from mankind. If a man touched it, he would die because he was made unclean through sin. Only the High Priest of Israel could enter near the mercy seat after being ceremonially clean.

The cherubim shall spread out their wings above, overshadowing the mercy seat with their wings, their faces one to another; toward the mercy seat shall the faces of the cherubim be. And you shall put the mercy seat on the top of the ark, and in the ark you shall put the testimony that I shall give you. There I will meet with you, and from above the mercy seat, from between the two cherubim that are on the ark of the testimony, I will speak with you about all that I will give you in commandment for the people of Israel. (Exodus 25:20–22)

He desired to speak to Israel with the promise to invite everyone to come near, experience his mercy and justice over sin, and dwell again in his presence one day. We can begin to see the connection between God's dwelling presence and inherent holiness.

A level of preservation of man's existence after Adam and Eve was allowed on Earth, albeit suffering and death would prevail for now. Man had allowed Satan to be the prince of the air — ruler of the age and the spiritual state of mankind, it would be only temporary. The power and gift of Adam's free will had seemingly dismantled God's plan, yet the Father was adamant that nothing would prevent the love of God from permanently dwelling with man again. Not even death. No length, height, or breadth of this universe and no angel or demon would separate us from the love of God in Christ Jesus, according to Romans 8:38.

The mercy of God would be found in Jesus Christ who was willing to die for the re-dwelling of his people. The wrath of the Father against sin and its partakers would be placed upon his Son Jesus.

Since, therefore, we have now been justified by his blood, much more shall we be saved by him from the wrath of God. For if while we were enemies we were reconciled to God by the death of his Son, much more, now that we are reconciled, shall we be saved by his life. (Romans 5:9–10)

This plan was not a Plan B. It was communicated within the Trinity before the world was created. The wrath was against sin. God was angry at its effect, and Christ was, too. So Jesus was to go on a mission to stand as the recipient of that wrath, and he would fulfill the plan willingly. This is mercy!

OUR IDENTITY FOUND IN A NAME

Mercy enables us to dwell with God. It carries an everlasting sustainable quality. But what happens in his presence? What happens with him dwelling with us, in us? The work of discipleship begins. We are transformed, purified, changed in the beauty of his presence. We are a new creation. We have a new name in Jesus Christ. We discover who we really are in him.

It may be a surprise to you, but the Great Commission spoken by Christ in *Matthew 28 – to "go therefore and make disciples of all nations, baptizing them in the name of the Father and of the Son and of the Holy Spirit, teaching them to observe all that I have commanded you"* — is not the first place of commission. The Great Commission started in Eden. Co-laboring with man begins in the Garden where Adam was called by God to name the animals and subdue the Earth. God would create them. Adam would label them. To name something in the Ancient Near East would mean to have authority over it.

Now out of the ground the LORD God had formed every beast of the field and every bird of the heavens and brought them to the man to see what he would call them. And whatever the man called every living creature, that was its name. (Genesis 2:19)

To name something is to know something about its function and its future.

Adam was entrusted to co-labor with God over his creation, which we will cover more in the last chapter. The enemy deceived Adam and Eve into believing God could not be trusted and they needed something else to be like God. They forgot that in their identity, they were already like God (Genesis 1:26). Their eyes of beholding the glory and beauty of God were lured and enticed to behold their own glory. In turn, they gave their God-given authority to Satan. The serpent seduced them with deception that led to worshiping a different ruler and kingdom — the kingdom of evil, through works and carnal flesh, the opposite of grace and holiness. Their purpose and provision that was found in dwelling with God was suddenly voided.

Adam and Eve — representing humankind — went from subduing, naming, and having dominion over the earth to worshiping it. They went from knowing their Father to being immediately separated. The close proximity to him was corrupted by disobedience. They had chosen to exalt themselves and take the things they thought they lacked or needed. Ultimately, it cost them their intimate dwelling with God.

Adam was meant to name the pieces of God's creation: animals, land formations, nature's processes. Instead, in many ways, they would end up naming and having dominion over him; generations followed under this suppression in the fashion of making idols and worshiping all that is created rather than the Creator. They went from dominion in describing function and form, class and order of the animal world to wandering in a wasteland of chaos, where the beasts they named would intimidate and often kill mankind. Adam and Eve went from mutually dwelling with creation to now living in fear and toiling with it. We, too, experience this when we are suppressed by the enemy's plans. Before sin entered their lives, the Father was their only comparison. Now, their eyes had been open to all things evil — things never designed to see like human death, jealousy, envy, and strife and with it, every fear and insecurity because of distance to God.

The lusts of the flesh rooted in a three-way cord of pride, fear, and shame would dominate mankind. They were no longer Father-conscious but suddenly self-conscious, aware of their nakedness, and had succumbed to the labels and thoughts of the accuser, Satan. Ruling, reigning, and naming with the Father had come to an end — at least temporarily. A paradise where beauty, goodness, truth, peace, and joy was once their environment had quickly become darkened. They now sensed the effects of shame, guilt, insecurity, exhaustion, worry, jealousness, and every ungodly belief perpetuated by fear and death. Their life, and the earth itself, was under a curse.

Mankind would continue by choice to live under many names and labels apart from the image and name God had given them. Their identity would be tainted. Their ability to behold the glory of God would suffer. But most of all, they would feel the deep separation from dwelling with their Father. They would be orphans by the choice of their disobedience. However, a longing and merciful pursuit to be reunited on the path of presence is the heart of the Father. Dwelling with his sons and daughters was always the beat of his heart. He would lead mankind on the path to hear his children cry "Abba!" again.

In order to rediscover our identity on the path of presence, we must lay all of our conscious and subconscious labels and self prescribed names found in sin at the foot of the cross, in the place of mercy and in the atonement of Jesus. If we in our sin could not dwell in God the Father's presence, we need to find someone who can help us return to its path. As we will see in the next chapter, receiving and believing the work of Christ will require humility and surrender for this very purpose. For the identity we reflect is not our own doings, it is the rescuing work of Jesus Christ.

SUMMARY

What do we learn from the place of the first mountain of Eden? God is a Father, who created you to dwell with him forever. His purpose in creating Paradise was for us to rule and reign with him on the Earth and extend its beauty, wisdom, and goodness for all to experience. In other words, you bear his image upon the Earth. The key to success was in the dwelling, the very presence of God, walking, talking, and communing with Adam and Eve. God has revealed himself as personal and relational, even within his own triune being.

He is secure, he is safe, he is provisional, and his abounding love is wrapped in an everlasting covenant, whereby a rich mercy would prevail. God withholds the wrath of the consequences of sin that came through Adam. Instead, he sent his son Jesus Christ, who shed his blood and gave his life so we could escape death and the separateness from the Father.

God loves gardens, and he loves to give. Being the ultimate Gardener, he would send the cultivator of life, Jesus, so that we could dwell in his presence again and holiness and humanity could be one. We have a renewed identity, no longer labeled and named by the things of our past — like fear, shame, and pride — but now, named righteous because of the just mercy of God. Jesus Christ has now become the Person in which our identity is found. Without him we only know death. But God provided a sacrifice for our death. It covered us and atoned for us. It had to be pure — clean and without sin — and it had to involve blood, the representation of life, and it would be Jesus' sinless blood and life required for our sin.

We are secure because Christ has overcome. We are righteous because Christ has become our righteousness. We are free from the enslaving sin of the world because Christ overcame the world. We can know the good attributes of the Father, and we can dwell with him, approach his holy throne — the place of his presence — because Jesus has made a pathway with his own life. Your identity as a disciple is Christ. We owe it all to him because he gave himself feely for us. This is the good news of the Bible and life today. This is Paradise — Eden! Let us continue in following Christ so that we may know how to dwell with and glorify him.

HUMILITY

Mount Moriah to Mount Golgotha

The life of blessing found in a posture of humility.

We now know something about the rich identity of the Father, the selfless union of the Trinity, and Christ's pursuit of us to dwell with us by his Holy Spirit. The pathway of the following chapters allows us to explore how we can walk in the identity of Christ and live as the full image in which God has created us. It starts with beholding the identity and glory of the person of Jesus Christ. Although they may be involved, the pathway of presence is not framed by our own opinions, emotions, experiences, or traditions. It is framed by the characteristics of the presence of God. His nature forms our identity. His words frame our identity. If God is our Creator and Father, then to know about ourselves is to first know him. This knowledge of God surpasses our limited intellect and total understanding. To know God is to experience him through relationship. As we will see, the only approach we take when experiencing God through relationship is through an attitude of humility — essentially the posture of submitting our will to the Lordship of Jesus and to the serving of others. How do we know if we have adopted that attitude or that that attitude has been formed in us? Well, the Bible gives us some pretty amazing examples of living this way that we can use as a guide on this path of presence.

MOUNT MORIAH

The mountain of identity leads us to our second mountain — the mountain of humility. It's one thing to understand the nature and identity of God, but it's another thing to embrace it or let him embrace you. There are two parts to our working definition of humility. The first is humility before God, shown in our surrender to Christ. The second is humility before others, displayed in our thoughts and actions toward other people. The second posture flows from the first.

The story of Abraham and his son Isaac at Mount Moriah is arguably the greatest Old Testament example of humility. Abraham shows us that in order to walk in our full identity in the image of God, we must walk in great humility. Before we get to Moriah, though, Abraham's story begins long before with a call from God to step out into the path of presence.

Now the LORD said to Abram, "Go from your country and your kindred and your father's house to the land that I will show you. And I will make of you a great nation, and I will bless you and make your name great, so that you will be a blessing." (Genesis 12:1–2)

Every disciple is called to step out into the path of presence. Abraham leaves a place of familiarity, his family, and his cultural and Babylonian spiritual identities to follow God — someone he doesn't know much about, except that he is true to his word. Abraham becomes a wanderer, comforted only by the words and presence of God. He learns to dwell in the wilderness of Canaan, a barren and desolate place. Abraham first shows us the humility of repentance.

THE HUMILITY IN REPENTANCE

Abraham is no peasant. He has influence, large flocks, servants, wealth, and a small army. He is known as a "lord." Yet what sets Abraham apart is his submission to God. He understands that he can do nothing of lasting value without him. God is the true source of all blessing and promise.

However, in the next chapter of Abraham's story, we see he takes matters into his own hands. His wife, Sarah, convinced him to take a surrogate (Hagar) to bear them a child because they had tried for many years to reproduce and nothing had happened. One chapter earlier, in Genesis 15:5, God had taken Abraham outside to look at the stars and said to him, "So shall your offspring be." The promise from God to Abraham had yet to come to pass — Abraham had no offspring — and Sarah's eyes saw a logical solution to fulfill the vision that God had ordained otherwise. Hagar bore a son to Abraham named Ishmael. Then, Sarah, the mastermind of this plan, forces Hagar and the child out into the wilderness because Hagar had begun to despise Sarah because Hagar was able to reproduce with Abraham. What a mess! This constructed attempt to produce a child of promise in the wisdom of their own eyes is foolishness in God's eyes. Abraham and Sarah are not alone. How many times do we contrive our own plans when we feel God is not near or working things out like he should?

Abraham was humbled and repented, and God was gracious and merciful. His promise was unconditional and not dependent on Abraham. Supernaturally, Abraham and Sarah did have a son, Isaac. Isaac was the son of promise and the fulfillment of what God had told them. Abraham's attitude of humility had begun to be developed by dwelling with God, waiting on his promises, watching his plan play out.

Humility produces a place where his Spirit can dwell.

For I know that nothing good dwells in me, that is, in my flesh. For I have the desire to do what is right, but not the ability to carry it out. (Romans 7:18)

> *"For my people are foolish;*
> *they know me not;*
> *they are stupid children;*
> *they have no understanding.*
> *They are 'wise' — in doing evil!*
> *But how to do good they know not." (Jeremiah 4:22)*

The first step in living a life of humility and blessing is found in our confession that we are foolish in our own strength, and not only that, but inherently evil. Our confession of our foolishness to God, and one another, allows the process of healing and of restoration to our true identity to take place.

THE HUMILITY TO TRUST

Abraham's journey toward a heart of humility had just begun though. Continuing to dwell with God on the path of presence grew his faith and developed his humility little by little. He understood his identity and his humble character began to form because of his proximity to God's presence. Finally, we come upon the story of Abraham at Mount Moriah in Genesis 22:3. Abraham is asked by God to offer his only son — the promised son, whom he loved — as a burnt offering. In ancient culture, child sacrifice was a common practice of worship to pagan gods, but never before asked for by Yahweh. The request of God brought a palpable sense of tension in Abraham, that the promise he was given was now "being asked to be given back." *Moriah* means "chosen by Jehovah," and was the same place Solomon built the Temple of God a few centuries later where animal sacrifices would be made according to the Law of Moses. Mount Moriah represents a chosen place of sacrifice. The life of a disciple always passes through the place of sacrifice, where every motive of the heart is purified and every possession and gift is tested and invited to be laid down and given back to God.

> ***Humility requires courage because it ultimately says, "I trust that you know better, God."***

When they came to the place of which God had told him, Abraham built the altar there and laid the wood in order and bound Isaac his son and laid him on the altar, on top of the wood. Then Abraham reached out his hand and took the knife to slaughter his son. But the angel of the LORD called to him from heaven and said, "Abraham, Abraham!" And he said, "Here I am." He said, "Do not lay your hand on the boy or do anything to him, for now I know that you fear God, seeing you have not withheld your son, your only son, from me." (Genesis 22:9–12)

As Abraham took steps toward obedience to God, the humility of his character shone. God, being good and the antithesis of the pagan deities of the day, then provided the animal offering and Isaac was preserved. Abraham knew God, so he feared God and in humility determined in his heart to obey the Creator. God then said, "Surely I will bless you and multiply your offspring because you obeyed My voice." In his obedience, Abraham reflected the very nature of God that put him to the test.

According to Romans 3:24–25 *we are justified by his grace as a gift, through the redemption that is in Christ Jesus, whom God put forward as a propitiation by his blood, to be received by faith. This was to show God's righteousness, because in his divine forbearance he had passed over former sins.*

Through Abraham's act, we see the foreshadowing of what God would do for mankind. He would send his only son, who would willingly lay down his own life as a sacrifice for our sins. Through the shedding of his blood and the resurrection of his body from the grave, he gives us the gift of life. God was essentially saying to Abraham, "Here I am! My presence is here with you. I will provide the offering."

Why die? Why blood? Why not just click his fingers so we could be in his presence again? The book of Romans tells us the penalty of sin is death (Rom 6:23). There had to be a death to cover that cost, and because God did not want humanity to pay that cost, he — in his wisdom — set up a way for that cost to be temporarily paid while the world waited for the ultimate and final payment in the death of Jesus on the cross.

Leviticus 17:11 says, *For the life of the flesh is in the blood, and I have given it for you on the altar to make atonement for your souls, for it is the blood that makes atonement by the life.*

Life is in the blood! That's why, in order for life to overcome death, blood of the body of flesh has to be given on the altar. If Christ came to fulfill the law (Matthew 5:17), then it would be no different. Blood would need to be shed. Abraham was commanded to stop short of offering his son up. God was showing Abraham that he is not like the gods of the world, who accept child sacrifice to appease their wrath. But God himself would take responsibility for the sin of man. Because only a sinless Man, who was also God, could provide the necessary sacrifice. It had to be Jesus (2 Corinthians 5:21, Romans 8:3–4).

And Abraham lifted up his eyes and looked, and behold, behind him was a ram, caught in a thicket by his horns. And Abraham went and took the ram and offered it up as a burnt offering instead of his son. So Abraham called the name of that place, "The LORD will provide"; as it is said to this day, "On the mount of the LORD it shall be provided." (Genesis 22:13–14)

Abraham remembered the goodness of God and entrusted him with every part of his life, even believing God would raise his son from the dead if needed (see Heb 11:19). If we are to be free and fulfilled in the presence of God, nothing can be withheld from him. Pride holds onto oneself; humility lets go. Abraham did not withhold his son, nor his heart from God and he showed his full trust in him.

Discipleship requires holding loosely to the things of this world and tightly to the character of God.

HUMILITY IN GIVING

The key words that God uses in response to Abraham's act of obedience are: "Seeing that you have not withheld..." Abraham did not withhold what he had. In regards to humbling ourselves in surrender, we can't ignore along the path of presence of how the Scriptures also talk about not withholding anything — especially our possessions. That's because God knows that our money and materiality is directly linked to our heart. Abraham exemplified this, too. If we are to be people of presence, we must have our hearts surrendered in every way, including not holding tightly to earthly possessions.

Do not lay up for yourselves treasures on earth, where moth and rust destroy and where thieves break in and steal, but lay up for yourselves treasures in heaven, where neither moth nor rust destroys and where thieves do not break in and steal. For where your treasure is, there your heart will be also. (Matthew 6:19–21)

Abraham was generous before he was asked to sacrifice Isaac. Before the law was even instituted regarding bringing a tithe (10% of income) to the temple, Abraham gave a tithe to Melchizedek, the Priest and King of Salem, and blessed him through the possessions he had won in battle (Genesis 14:16). The king has no genealogy or ancestral line, but he represents a type of Christ as the eternal Priest and King of the New Jerusalem (see Heb 7:1-10). Giving to Melchizedek symbolized blessing Jesus Christ. The precedence also shows us that the law was never sufficient to achieve what God desired — hearts that choose to be cheerful and generous, not just because God has required it. Money is neutral, but in the hands of the righteous it can bless others. In the hands of the wicked, it can bring destruction. Jesus knew money had the power to grip us, for Satan had tempted him with riches and glory of earthly kingdoms. Jesus reminded his disciples that you cannot serve both God and money.

No one can serve two masters, for either he will hate the one and love the other, or he will be devoted to the one and despise the other. You cannot serve God and money. (Matthew 6:24)

Sowing and reaping is a principle established by God's word in the Old and New Testaments to show our love and trust in him. It ensures the needs of others are met. If God is to have all of us, he must know that we can be givers in every way.

Abraham proved that the Lord was his provider by blessing others and by giving up his greatest possession, his son. Other than God, nothing would be his master, no relationship or material possession or false ideology.

We see from the Mount of Moriah that obedience and humility are required in order for God's presence to dwell. His presence is found in the costly place of sacrifice. His presence will ask of us to turn from the knowledge of our own ways and acknowledge that he is higher and all-knowing. Abraham left what he knew and followed the voice of God. He understood the source of his blessing and entrusted his life, and his son's life, to the secure presence of God, and God blessed him. Humility enabled Abraham to walk in the righteous identity and provisional nature of God. Through Abraham's sacrifice, the people and land of Israel were also cleansed and made holy for God to dwell.

MOUNT GOLGOTHA

Abraham is an incredible example of the attitude of humility that works in those who spend time listening to God's voice and who walk the path of his presence, trusting his provision. Abraham's act would foreshadow God giving his only Son as an eternal sacrifice for mankind.

The ultimate example in humility is Jesus Christ himself. The humility that adjusts our lens and perspective and corresponding behaviors as we walk the path of presence patterns the attitude with which Jesus lived and operated his entire life. The culmination of his life of humility was demonstrated for the world to see up on a mountain outside of Jerusalem where he gave up his life for the salvation of humanity.

The mountain of Golgotha, Skull Rock, is the trek where we find the highest example of humility. Perhaps "humiliation" is a better description, from the same Latin root. Golgotha was more known as a hill in the New Testament than a mountain — the place where Jesus was crucified.

Golgotha means "the place of skull." It refers to death. Death was never the intention for man. It was brought about through Satan's pride, and ultimately, man's disobedience. Dead things were considered unclean and not fit for the presence of God. In the Old Testament, no man who was unclean, who had touched the dead, or had not ceremonially washed could come near God.

However, death was needed if life was going to be restored. Life would not end in death, but death was the valley that Jesus needed to pass through if life was going to be experienced for all, because life is in the blood (Leviticus 17).

What shall we say then? Are we to continue in sin that grace may abound? By no means! How can we who died to sin still live in it? Do you not know that all of us who have been baptized into Christ Jesus were baptized into his death? We were buried therefore with him by baptism into death, in order that, just as Christ was raised from the dead by the glory of the Father, we too might walk in newness of life. (Romans 6:1–4)

If we are in Christ Jesus and he is our Lord, then we have been baptized into his death. The pathway of discipleship requires dying — maybe not a physical dying (although many will be martyred for their faith) — but dying to ourselves, our sinful desires, the pride of our own ambitions, our agendas, our insecurities, our rights, and also our need to be right.

There is no true life without passing through death — the dying to self.

There is no ability to walk in the image of God without dying to yourself. There is no ability to know his presence when you are the center and lord of your own life. There is no ability to find true peace, joy, and love if you have not first been spiritually buried and baptized with Christ. There is no salvation without humility. There is no forgiveness for sin without humbling your life and confessing your sinful nature at the foot of the cross.

This might sound strange, but dying is the key to living! The above passage in Romans 6:4 says, "in order that" — forecasting something coming after death, which is the newness of life!

THE HUMILITY OF JESUS

For God so loved the world, that he gave his only Son, that whoever believes in him should not perish but have eternal life. For God did not send his Son into the world to condemn the world, but in order that the world might be saved through him. (John 3:16–17)

Mercy was on full display. He came down and stooped low as a gift to mankind. The Holy Spirit would also convict the world of its unrighteous state, not condemn it for those who believe (see Romans 8:1). Satan condemns us, but God lovingly convicts us of our sin. To those who would humbly believe in the merciful One, mercy would be shown.

For judgment is without mercy to one who has shown no mercy.

Mercy triumphs over judgment. (James 2:13)

Just as Abraham believed in God and his provision, we, too, must believe in Jesus Christ and his sacrifice. Humility is necessary for salvation. You cannot earn salvation. You cannot work your way to freedom. You must simply believe and follow Jesus as Lord and Savior.

Because, if you confess with your mouth that Jesus is Lord and believe in your heart that God raised him from the dead, you will be saved. (Romans 10:9)

God desires that we call upon his name and cry out for help and the renewal of our souls. Come, save me, forgive me, I need you, lead me — these are all words of faith that enable us to experience the grace and peace and joy of our Father. We stand, justified before him, only because he looks at us through the life of his Son, Jesus. We are made holy, and only holiness can approach him. Christ's salvation has enabled us to dwell again forever with God — the Father, Son, and Holy Spirit. The perfect peace of his presence is with us, and nothing can take him from us!

Therefore, since we have been justified by faith, we have peace with God through our Lord Jesus Christ. Through him we have also obtained access by faith into this grace in which we stand, and we rejoice in hope of the glory of God. (Romans 5:1–2)

Faith in the work of Jesus upon the cross justifies you to receive grace! You have been acquitted of guilt and shame in order to enter his peace. Receiving Jesus meant receiving him, the "person-if-ication" of peace, not just a feeling of quiet or calm. Christ, the person of God, filled your life with hope, glory, peace, and grace because this is who he is.

For I am sure that neither death nor life, nor angels nor rulers, nor things present nor things to come, nor powers, nor height nor depth, nor anything else in all creation, will be able to separate us from the love of God in Christ Jesus our Lord. (Romans 8:38–39)

This is the greatest reassurance of his presence. When we repent — turn to Jesus and confess our need for him — nothing can get between us and the love of God, not even angels.

THE HUMILITY IN BAPTISM

The pathway of presence leads to water — a need for our lives to be immersed, or baptized. It is a necessary next step for any new disciple who longs to follow Jesus in obedience. Matthew 28 instructs us to make disciples and baptize them in the name of the Father, Son, and Holy Spirit. Water was viewed as ceremonially cleansing. When we go down into the waters of baptism, it symbolizes how the old person of self and sinfulness has died with Christ. When we come up out of the waters, it demonstrates the newness of life found in Christ's resurrection. It's a public declaration of the inner saving faith that has occurred through the Holy Spirit when we first believed that Jesus is Lord.

But why did Jesus have to get baptized? Wasn't he perfect and sinless? The answer is yes, but Jesus is taking it a step further.

Then Jesus came from Galilee to the Jordan to John, to be baptized by him. John would have prevented him, saying, "I need to be baptized by you, and do you come to me?" But Jesus answered him, "Let it be so now, for thus it is fitting for us to fulfill all righteousness." Then he consented. (Matthew 3:13–15)

Jesus had to fulfill all righteousness. His posture to be baptized symbolized the mystery that he identified with sinners, yet was sinless. Sinners could never fulfill the requirements of the law of Moses, but Jesus could. In regards to baptism, John the Baptist was from the line of priests of Levi. The Levites' role was to present sacrifices to God on behalf of the people. When Jesus came to him, John said that he was not worthy to baptize a spotless lamb (see Luke 3:16), yet Jesus humbled himself to John's baptism so that Jesus could fulfill his priestly role as the one who was righteous, serving all mankind to become their sacrifice.

The humility of Christ to be baptized made way for us to identify with his life as righteous.

Therefore, if anyone is in Christ, he is a new creation. The old has passed away; behold, the new has come. (2 Corinthians 5:17)

The baptism of Jesus Christ displays a beautiful humility and selfless picture of the serving Trinity. In the act of salvation through Jesus, we hear the words of the Father, declaring, "This is my beloved Son, with whom I am well pleased," (Matthew 3:17). The Father is sharing his intentional love for the Son as well as his own love for mankind from before the foundation of the world (Ephesians 1:4). Jesus is sent by the Father (1 John 4:14) and the Holy Spirit descends upon Jesus when he is baptized. The Holy Spirit remains on him for the purpose of his ministry and convicting the world of its sin (John 16:8). The Holy Spirit always points and leads us to Christ. When we know Christ, we can be reconciled to the Father as a new creation. The Father sees you as new, not your old sinful man.

The pathway of presence is not all goosebumps and cotton candy, as we have seen. It is holy, beautiful, and glorious to be in the presence of Jesus. And because it is holy, it means he will also refine you. He will deal with the old you and see that it is buried. He will continually sanctify you — meaning, the Holy Spirit will purify you — so that you remain in him and walk in his image. Why? Because he wants your presence walking with his presence.

THE COST OF HUMILITY

An attitude of humility produces a life that can walk along the path of presence, but with this glorious revelation of the character of God — and the character that we are developing — dwelling in his presence comes a cost. The cost and richness of the transformative presence and work of Jesus is invoked in Paul's letter to the Galatians. If we are to be dwelling places for the divine presence of God to make his union within our lives, then spiritual crucifixion is the only pathway.

I have been crucified with Christ. It is no longer I who live, but Christ who lives in me. And the life I now live in the flesh I live by faith in the Son of God, who loved me and gave himself for me. (Galatians 2:20)

There's a cost to following Jesus, and the cost is great. It's a cost many people are unwilling to pay. It's the cost of "no longer living to self," surrendering your life for his. The apostle Paul understood as a disciple that the former "I" was crucified, the old inner self of sin representing the flesh died and no longer lives.

What's it like to be crucified? Literally, it means to impale or to drive down with stakes. Symbolically speaking, with Christ, it means the passions of our selfishness must continually be submitted to the work of the cross. They must die and be destroyed. This is why humility is imperative. Disciples who are dead in Christ don't get offended. You can't offend someone who's already dead. The "old sinful man" would, but the "new man of the spirit" doesn't. We are not immune to hurt, yet offense doesn't stick. The new life has the voice of the Holy Spirit speaking and showing us the model example of what Jesus did. If we are in Christ we must forgive because he forgave us. We must die to bitterness, revenge, and anger and conform to the image of Jesus with the help of the Holy Spirit. Humility leads to true identity in Jesus.

Along the path of presence in following Jesus, you crucified your rights to be right. You crucified your need to be seen as valuable by the world's standards. You crucified your need for acceptance from unhealthy relationships. You crucified the thoughts that you are undeserving, insecure, and unworthy of God's grace. That person — that "you" — no longer lives. You crucified your lack of self-control, foul language, outbursts of anger and rage. You crucified your need to lie and justify yourself before others. You crucified your desire to be the most important person in the room or desire to be in the public spotlight. You died to your ego, your social status, and wanting to be liked. You crucified what others think of you. You crucified fear and worry about the future. You crucified procrastination and laziness. You crucified being controlled by lust and addictions. You submitted your sexuality to God. You laid your life down and picked up Christ's holy and perfect way. In doing so and counting the cost, you experience the Kingdom of God and his ways, his presence.

Jesus answered him, "Truly, truly, I say to you, unless one is born again he cannot see the kingdom of God." (John 3:3)

Still want to follow Jesus? Many times we are not informed of that kind of cost, but when we read his word, we clearly see that Jesus tells those who desire to follow him to leave everything behind.

God has given you a unique personality. You don't lose your created distinctiveness and gifts and become a robot. But as you walk out the pathway of discipleship you should no longer talk, think, or act in any way like the former person you used to be, who was dead in sin. You surrendered your gifts, your talents, your thoughts, your dreams, and your desires to Jesus. When you humbled yourself to make him Lord, you said, "You are my desire. May your desires become mine." You have been born again and justified with a new position in Christ. You have a new set of values and priorities, and the process of being sanctified — or being made whole — to be like Christ "is" and "has" begun!

"Follow me, and I will make you fishers of men." Immediately, they left their nets and followed him. (Matthew 4:19-20)

This passage symbolizes leaving your past life behind. Leaving your "nets" as a disciple of Christ means leaving your comforts and the familiarities of an old way of life. Everything associated with your identity changes when you no longer live. You are a son or daughter of God first — a Christ follower, a Christian. What you do with your skills or with your knowledge and education is always secondary to your true identity. The world might identify you as a businessman, a doctor, lawyer, athlete, janitor, or a mechanic, but these are only fields of work we have applied ourselves in. You are first a son or daughter and an ambassador of Jesus Christ (2 Corinthians 5:20). An ambassador simply represents someone more important than themselves. Can we go a little further? Jesus really made it clear what it takes to follow him:

If anyone comes to me and does not hate his own father and mother and wife and children and brothers and sisters, yes, and even his own life, he cannot be my disciple. Whoever does not bear his own cross and come after me cannot be my disciple. For which of you, desiring to build a tower, does not first sit down and count the cost, whether he has enough to complete it? Otherwise, when he has laid a foundation and is not able to finish, all who see it begin to mock him, saying, "This man began to build and was not able to finish." (Luke 14:26–30)

Hate? A clue is found rather in the Hebrew understanding of this word that tells us that we must love second — or love less — every other relationship compared to our love for God. We see this in Genesis 29:30–31 when Jacob "hated" Leah and loved Rachel. Rachel was his first love, and Leah would always be his second love.

A Roman cross symbolized humiliation, not just punishment, as the ultimate physical and emotional tormenting of one's life. Jesus says if you're not willing to take up your own individual cross, bearing humiliation from others and the humiliation of your own sinful flesh, there is no way you can follow him. Jesus said this because this was the path that he would take. If you want to emulate Jesus and be in his presence, you must follow his presence, while being sustained by his presence through suffering, pain, and humiliation. It may seem long, yet it is really only for a little while:

Resist him, firm in your faith, knowing that the same kinds of suffering are being experienced by your brotherhood throughout the world. And after you have suffered a little while, the God of all grace, who has called you to his eternal glory in Christ, will himself restore, confirm, strengthen, and establish you. To him be the dominion forever and ever. Amen. (1 Peter 5:9–11)

If suffering is not an accepted part in the discipleship process, we are deceived into thinking everything should be easy, without pain, struggle, offense, and hurt. And so we begin on the path, only to get so far and turn around because we did not first count the cost. Our lives reflect an unfinished building in ruins, instead of a house that hosts his glory and presence.

Although he was a son, he learned obedience through what he suffered. And being made perfect, he became the source of eternal salvation to all who obey him. (Hebrews 5:8–9)

For Jesus, suffering precedes perfection. Though he was perfect in the sense of being sinless, he was also being made perfect through obedience. Sacrificial obedient suffering is how the goal of salvation for mankind is reached. The manner in which Christ came to this Earth displays the true meaning of perfection. We learn humility through suffering, and when we walk in obedience, we are walking perfectly like Jesus.

It may seem like we are giving up so much that we come out in deficit or we are losing out. The lies of the enemy would have you believe that God is not enough. This was the lie that Adam and Eve believed in the Garden. What we lay down does not compare to what we receive. Jesus does not lead us to lack or places of shame and doubt, just like we've seen from the Father. Jesus leads us into the beauty of truth. True freedom, true peace, and true joy are received. You are not losing; you are gaining true life.

Paul knew of this in the world and in Heaven with Jesus:

For to me to live is Christ, and to die is gain. (Philippians 1:21)

For freedom Christ has set us free; stand firm therefore, and do not submit again to a yoke of slavery. (Galatians 5:1)

Are you no longer living, is Christ living within you? Are you no longer bound by the past, dictated to by sin and labels of the world, and trapped in the trauma of life's experiences? Are you free in Christ from the curse of sin? Are you carrying around baggage from years ago? The good news is you no longer have to!

Humble yourself to Jesus Christ. Listen to his words, obey them, and follow them, for they are life. Lay aside your pride and what you think is best, and trust him. Walk in the pathway of his presence that is blessed because he is found there.

THE HUMILITY OF MEEK LIVING

Why all this humble talk? Well, it is for good reason. The only time we see Jesus Christ describe his character is in Matthew 11. Jesus could have said, I am powerful, I am wise and intelligent, I am perfect, and all of that would have been true. But to describe himself, he uses the words "gentle" and "lowly in heart." Other translations use the words "humble" and "meek." We should take serious note if we desire to become like him.

Take my yoke upon you, and learn from me, for I am gentle and lowly in heart, and you will find rest for your souls. For my yoke is easy, and my burden is light. (Matthew 11:29–30)

When Jesus is talking about a yoke, he is not talking about breakfast, but rather he is talking about his teaching and his way of life. It is not an easy life, but his way is light. It is good — the best, not like the Pharisees and religious teachers, whose teaching was oppressive and too burdensome to uphold. Jesus connects great rest in our lives to accepting the teaching of grace and mercy found in the truth of learning to live humbly. Jesus could find rest because he was submitted to his Father's words in humility. If we are walking heavy and burdened by the cares of the world, there is hope for us to walk in revelation, to walk in the light, and to carry words of hope — not the burden of hopelessness.

Gentleness and meekness don't sound like the descriptors of a mighty warrior or a type of leader that people would want to follow. But Jesus is showing us the key to true strength. Meekness is not void of strength, but full of strength under restraint.

Meekness rests in placing our strength in Jesus' sovereignty.

The presence of God is attracted to meekness because within this attribute, there is no self or flesh attempting to prove that our strengths and abilities are worth something. There is no fight for glory. There is a difference between absorbing glory and reflecting it. Absorbing glory will lead to our downfall. We were not designed for it. We, who are in Christ, are to reflect him and give him glory.

Jesus could be gentle with those around him because he was led by the Spirit, not just of his own divine nature. The Father sent the Holy Spirit from Heaven which descended upon Jesus — who, as he grew, was keenly aware of where his power came from.

Do you not believe that I am in the Father and the Father is in me? The words that I say to you I do not speak on my own authority, but the Father who dwells in me does his works. Believe me that I am in the Father and the Father is in me, or else believe on account of the works themselves. (John 14:10–11)

Jesus didn't react or try to usurp every accusation or opinion about him. Most times, he kept quiet. Even in his crucifixion, they would mock him and ask him to rescue himself off the cross (Mark 15:31). But meekness doesn't need to respond with self-assertiveness; it yields to the Father's identity. The Father would defend him, and raise him up. Jesus didn't have to prove himself because he was led and esteemed by his Father's words and instructions. This was his key to life: living in meekness and humility.

Philippians 2:3–8 reiterates the posture of Christ:

Do nothing from selfish ambition or conceit, but in humility count others more significant than yourselves. Let each of you look not only to his own interests, but also to the interests of others. Have this mind among yourselves, which is yours in Christ Jesus, who, though he was in the form of God, did not count equality with God a thing to be grasped, but emptied himself, by taking the form of a servant, being born in the likeness of men. And being found in human form, he humbled himself by becoming obedient to the point of death, even death on a cross.

"Though he was in the form of God" — that is, Jesus was God. But he did not grasp or seize the power that was accessible to him in his own divinity as the Son who took on a human nature. Jesus restricted himself with human limitations, divested himself of his rights, lost none of his inner value or divinity being God, yet veiled his outer glory in the form of a servant. Jesus was perfectly emptied. He was empty because he came not to be served but to serve. And he was perfect through the accomplishment of giving his life as a ransom for many (Mark 10:45).

If we look at Adam in the Garden, his actions were like Satan before him. He tried to grasp becoming equal with God, and in doing so, he forfeited his inheritance and was separated from God's presence. He was already made in the image of God, in his uniqueness he still was deceived into believing the accusative voice of Satan. Unbelief causes us to grasp at all kinds of things to substitute the blessing we have in Christ. Jesus, on the other hand, was equal with God. He was God, and yet he chose not to grasp all of the glory available to him. By not grasping all power, his humility to go to the cross made way for our inheritance and perfect reconciliation.

Our moral perfection with God can be defined as humility to the point of death, or dying to self. Only then can his glory be revealed through us. We can be perfect (Matthew 5:48) as Jesus even commands. There is no pride in Christ — only strength under self control. It's exemplified on the hill of Golgotha, where Jesus submitted his will to the Father — just as it was for Abraham on Mount Moriah.

Humility = Jesus stooped to Earth

It is observed that Jesus didn't lose anything. He added, as emphasized by the participle, "by taking on" the form of a servant. This is a challenge to the secular perception of servanthood and humility as a form of weakness. We never lose. We add with humility. The implications are convicting for us as disciples in our walk and character with others.

THE HUMILITY OF PREFERRING OTHERS

"Have this mind" — that is, the example of Jesus. We, in humility, are to consider "others more significant" than ourselves. The words to the Philippians are strong. "Do nothing out of selfish ambition."

It's impossible to be a disciple of Jesus and be narcissistic. Though at times we can struggle, there's a difference between a healthy love of self or a confident view of the image we are created in and a self-absorbing insecurity or naivety. How much of this world lives in selfish ambition? The truth is, we all have. But remember, you have died and now Christ lives in you. You are a new creation. The new creation is led by the Spirit of God, who serves others and learns to think about others more than the needs of yourself.

Preference Christianity doesn't exist in the terms of I, me, and myself. Only, them, they, and us. Discipleship must take place in the context of community.

If we are in the presence of Jesus, he will ask us to reconcile ourselves to one another by continually putting on humility.

This requires an intentional lowering of self that only the Holy Spirit can help us with, if we are willing.

The Apostle Paul wants us to understand that we need to embrace the reality that we are "members of one another" (Romans 12:5) because Christ has made us one in him.

Part of the significance and symbolism of being baptized in water is that it shows that we became immersed into one body of people, deeply tethered to one another.

For in one Spirit we were all baptized into one body — Jews or Greeks, slaves or free — and all were made to drink of one Spirit. For the body does not consist of one member but of many. (1 Corinthians 12:13–14)

It takes humility to submit to a body of strangers — people who are different from you and who don't talk, look, dress, or think like you do. Think about all the diverse people that Jesus interacted with, from the religious to the businessman to the naked demoniac to the woman at the well, and also children. Jesus came to serve others, to seek and save every kind of lost person. We must break out of our prejudices if we are to be true disciples. The Holy Spirit must be allowed to convict us of attitudes of pride and judgment.

The path of discipleship walks hand-in-hand with others who carry the image of God. That's everyone — every tribe, nation, and ethnicity. This is part of our refining process. God allows others to help shape and refine our hearts to grow in maturity to the fullness of Christ (Ephesians 4:13). We can learn much about Jesus through others. We cannot afford to forfeit the lessons he is trying to show us in the people we interact with. There is an opportunity for his glory and his presence to be revealed.

Ultimately to love Jesus is to love others. Humility doesn't work in isolation from others. There is great protection from wandering, counsel, encouragement, support, and friendship when we consider others more significant than ourselves. The attribute of humility has amazing preserving qualities for your life's journey that will bless others and allow God to exalt you.

Likewise, you who are younger, be subject to the elders. Clothe yourselves, all of you, with humility toward one another, for "God opposes the proud but gives grace to the humble."

Humble yourselves, therefore, under the mighty hand of God so that at the proper time he may exalt you, casting all your anxieties on him, because he cares for you. (1 Peter 5:5–7)

God hates pride because he knows what it does to his children. We become idols unto ourselves. Worshiping our own deified imaginations and knowledge. We fail to become the image we were created in, and we are deceived into creating our own image, just like the Israelites did (see Exodus 32:4).

Internally, creating our own image produces more confusion and chaos, resulting in unwanted pressures to become the solution to all things. Anxiety and worry are compounded from the fear of an inability to control situations or thoughts. When we are the lord of our own lives, we are trying to control external circumstances and the fears of life that seem overwhelming — which is a good reason why Peter connected humility with casting our anxieties on God.

We were never meant to control the "what if's" of life, but in humility, cast upon Jesus our thoughts and our future, enabling him to lead us into his peace and truth.

If there is a direct correlation between living in anxiety and isolating ourselves and our thoughts, then there is a direct correlation between living in peace and rest by living in humility and surrender to God. God has promised us his Holy Spirit, who leads us in self-control — including in our thoughts. We can live in victory because we have been given access to the mind of Christ (1 Corinthians 2:16). If we ask and meditate on his words, we can think Christ-like thoughts because we are in him as new creations awakened to his Spirit and words. Surrendered thinking allows God to renew our minds of old thought patterns about him, ourselves, and those around us. (More on that in the next chapter).

Finally, our Father's desire is to honor you as he did with his Son Jesus.

> *Before destruction a man's heart is haughty,*
> *but humility comes before honor. (Proverbs 18:12)*

Pride will result in falling, but humility will allow God to exalt you among men and women for his glory. Self promotion is not needed. God sees you like he saw Abraham and like he saw Hagar with a desire to bless. Self-exalting pride destroys the identity of who you are. Confession, vulnerability, and transparency allow God to save us, secure us, and sustain us.

Fearing man and attempting to please those around you will stifle the will of God for your life. We are called to serve others, not to please them through fear. There is nothing more important than pleasing your Father in Heaven. Remember his words spoken over Jesus: "My loved one, in whom I am well pleased." Humility is a significant key in abiding in his presence. To walk in the path of Jesus is to walk in humility. Let him lead you.

SUMMARY

Christ displayed the ultimate example and reality of humility on Golgotha in the emptying himself of all self-seeking desire. He was obedient to the point of death. Greater than Abraham, who also did not withhold, and led his son Isaac on Mount Moriah, God, too, would provide the sacrifice. Jesus followed the perfect will of his Father to the cross. He fulfilled the mission for which he was sent. He humbled himself under his mighty hand and was dependent on the Holy Spirit to serve others and to be sustained until the end. He walked with a disposition of meekness and gentleness. Not one hint of arrogance or pride or insecurity came from him. His only delight was to please the Father. In his success with not grasping the powers available in him, he went to the cross to die for you and me. His life was crucified for our freedom, and Paul reminds us that in the crucified life we are called to, dwells the unfathomable union of Christ's Spirit within our bodies. The Father exalted him and raised him from the dead to sit at his right hand in Heaven. Jesus walked out his mission in his identity as the Son of God because he humbled himself. His words, "Father, if you are willing, remove this cup from me. Nevertheless, not my will, but yours, be done," (Luke 22:42) continue to be the echoes and power of humility in Jesus we are to example today along the path of presence.

INTIMACY

Mount Sinai to the Mount of Olives

*Conscious closeness nurtured
through covenant.*

Our journey has started with understanding God's nature and identity. We have witnessed him as Father, we have seen his desire to walk and talk with mankind as he did with Adam in the Garden. He is personal — a God who shares his presence, who longs to dwell with his people. Our identity is found in him and in his purpose for us — that is, to walk in his image of steadfast love, truth, righteousness, justice, holiness, and mercy. This is integral, as we will see later on, to establish his purposes to co-labor in serving the nations through the presence of the Holy Spirit, extending the goodness of the Kingdom of God found in his Son and King Jesus Christ. We are ambassadors of Christ who gave his life for us that we may live and glorify him. Jesus is the center of our existence and the sole reason we have been saved from sin. He desires to become our Savior, Lord, King, and friend. We can be friends of God!

In order to embrace the identity we have been created in, humility and meekness is required. The right to become sons and daughters and the power to live in his presence as overcomers cannot be found without surrendering our whole lives to Jesus. Lordship requires dying to ourselves, a removal of our own throne and crowns, and accepting Christ's rule and reign. Apart from him, we can do nothing of eternal value. He calls each one of us to leave our familiar way of life and walk worthy of the image we were made in.

When identity is known and when humility to Jesus is our posture, then intimacy can be birthed. The sweet fragrance of surrendering produces closeness, a knowing, and a drawing near to God the Father as he first drew near to us. The possibilities of relationship can be reconciled. Innocence and intimacy that was lost in the Garden — cut off and separated from God — can now be restored. Man can once again abide permanently with the Spirit of God. We have been made whole and new through Christ to access intimacy to the Father. Christ's holiness has become ours. We have died with

Christ, and we have been raised with him, experiencing the beauty and reality of the glory Adam and Eve once knew.

And this is eternal life, that they know you, the only true God, and Jesus Christ whom you have sent. (John 17:3)

It's an amazing thought that we could know something about God, that we could breathe his name, that he would invite us into his being and presence, that we could talk, listen, and hear his voice speaking to us and through us. As disciples, we have been called to a life of intimacy with God. To walk every day knowing him, growing in him, and glorifying him. As a reminder, this is what we will be doing with God forever:

And I heard a loud voice from the throne saying, "Behold, the dwelling place of God is with man. He will dwell with them, and they will be his people, and God himself will be with them as their God." (Revelation 21:3)

Intimacy is the word *Yada* in the Hebrew language of the Old Testament. It is a verb meaning "to know." It is one of the most descriptive relational words there is. Between man and woman it speaks of a deep tethering of heart, soul, and body. The verb suggests more than cerebral ideals but also experiential knowing. It is knowing through living. It is to be deeply acquainted with the inner heart of a person through experience. Intimacy is not easy to accept for some. It involves love, and love is vulnerable. It requires a devoted transparency — the sharing of our heart and personal thoughts, desires, and struggles.

There is a necessary vulnerability required for intimacy, and there can be no hiding.

That is why when Adam and Eve disobeyed God, the first thing they did was hide. Innocence and relationship to God were lost. Shame and guilt and fear causes us to cover up and suppress the naked vulnerability of our hearts. It stifles the emotions we were made with, causing us to run from the intimacy God desires. Sin causes us to run from the presence of God and hides our image.

Intimacy is not guaranteed just because we are present or around people. In the case of God's plan, he created the gift of sex for enjoyment, pleasure, and procreation. In the Bible, sexual intimacy was what marked a covenant between husband and wife. It was symbolic of yielding your whole self, even your body to your spouse. Yet even when there is sexual activity, there is no guarantee that intimacy is present. Just because we have heard or read something about God does not mean we know him. In our relationship with God, he desires every part of us: spirit (the place he communicates with), soul (the mind, will, and emotions), and body (our physical flesh) to be set apart. Yes, even our bodies can glorify God and are to be presented as living sacrifice, holy and acceptable to God (Romans 12:1). God wants your whole life. To love God is to love him with everything.

You shall love the LORD your God with all your heart and with all your soul and with all your might. (Deuteronomy 6:5)

Does God have your whole heart? Your whole soul? All of your mind and strength? Or just your Sunday or part of your lifestyle? The Bible tells us that the only way we can truly love God is with everything — our possessions, family, children, and jobs. Time and resources were given to you to love God. We know this to be true from the way he loved us. Jesus gave it all. God desires to make your life a vessel where your body, soul, and spirit can become a home for him to dwell in — a place to make an abode, not just visit occasionally. A spirit requires a willing mind and body to inhabit. Many are entertaining all kinds of evil spirits. Some people do this knowingly while other people are naive to it. God designed us to host his Holy Spirit within us.

MOUNT SINAI

That leads us to the tabernacling presence of God with man in the Old Testament where his desires to dwell were illustrated. The story of God dwelling with Israel begins with Moses. The significance of Mount Sinai is where we journey to on the pathway of presence.

And let them make me a sanctuary, that I may dwell in their midst. Exactly as I show you concerning the pattern of the tabernacle, and of all its furniture, so you shall make it. (Exodus 25:8-9)

Tabernacle means "to dwell," from the Hebrew word *miskan*. God desired a dwelling place where his glory could dwell with Moses and his chosen people, the Israelites. The first instruction he gave Moses was to build him a tent. It was a lavish tent with materials, curtains, and vessels, all symbolizing aspects of his character and ways. It would be holy, or set apart. Each item was intentionally selected and anointed with oil, consecrated, and made pure. Sweet smelling incense filled the inside of the tent, covering any pollution of man or scent of death. It would be called the Tent of Meeting, where God would meet with humanity on a regular basis. The most intimate place was the last of three compartments of the tent, called the Holy of Holies.

All of Israel would encamp around the tent of the Lord. The Levites and priests camped nearest to the Tabernacle as a ring of protection with each of the twelve tribes pitching their tents around them in North, South, East, and West positions. God was right in the midst of his people. But only Moses could enter the Holy of Holies, or the inner chamber. He acted as the High Priest, a mediator on behalf of the people, communicating God's words and heart to the people.

Then Moses and Aaron, Nadab, and Abihu, and seventy of the elders of Israel went up, and they saw the God of Israel. There was under his feet as it were a pavement of sapphire stone, like the very heaven for clearness. And he did not lay his hand on the chief men of the people of Israel; they beheld God, and ate and drank. (Exodus 24:9–11)

Wow! They beheld the glory of God, eating, drinking, and communing from the base of the Mountain of God, Mount Sinai/Horeb. They were clothed in a cloud of fire and smoke that represented his presence and purifying nature. God withheld his anger at their sin. God showed his divine hospitality, complete with a meal, even outside the most intimate setting which was on top of the mountain. His kindness proved to be inclusive to others.

The sapphire speaks of the foundation gem stones of clarity and purity found in God and the New Heavens and Earth, literally meaning the Tabernacle of God where Heaven is on Earth (Revelation 21:19). The structure of the Tabernacle — and later the Temple — shares a symbolic framework to that of the boundaries and details of the Garden of Eden. In its most intimate setting, Eden contained a garden with the Tree of Life. This was the holy of holies — a place where God's presence would manifestly be seen and known upon the mercy seat. The rest of Eden would serve as the holy place where mankind was designed to minister, just as priests would worship and host the glory of God in the Tabernacle. The Levites would also guard the Tabernacle, standing between people's sin and God's holiness, just as the cherubim did at the edge of the Garden.

The outer place, or courts, was a space for God's people to offer sacrifices and be made clean, washed with water and made right before him. It pertained to the outer regions of Eden in which a river flowed out from the east. It symbolized the design for the Earth to be cultivated, to look like the garden of paradise, nourishing and extending the glory and value of God to the rest of the world he had created.

The Tabernacle, and later a Temple, was most importantly built to foreshadow the final or (eschatological) dwelling place of the New Eden/Heaven and Earth that contains the sanctuary of Christ's presence. Revelation 21 reveals that the entire house or temple of God will be the cosmos of a new creation — not just a building on Earth, which is unable to contain his presence.

The greater and more perfect tent exists in the heavenly sanctuary: the New Heaven and New Earth. The Tabernacle and Temple in Israel's history are only a shadow or microcosm of the greater Tabernacle of presence we are to enter.

INTIMACY WITH HIS VOICE

Whenever Moses went out to the tent, all the people would rise up, and each would stand at his tent door, and watch Moses until he had gone into the tent. When Moses entered the tent, the pillar of cloud would descend and stand at the entrance of the tent, and the LORD would speak with Moses. (Exodus 33:8–9)

The Lord would speak with Moses within a tent — the dwelling place of God on earth. Only Moses was invited to come further up the mountain to a more intimate place. The elders remained at the lower regions. God was sharing his ways to a man set apart to lead God's people. He was foreshadowing a time when God could dwell with every individual. In the meantime, God had established a sacrificial system through Moses, that by the blood of an animal — a substitute — offered on an altar before the tabernacle, the people could approach God. Through this sacrifice, communion with God was possible. God spoke to Moses several thousand years ago, and God is still speaking to his people today as Lord and friend! We will see as we read on how this is possible.

Thus the LORD used to speak to Moses face to face, as a man speaks to his friend. (Exodus 33:11a)

The place God speaks from tells us more about who he is and the means in which we are required to approach him. We know the word describes God speaking here using "face" as a figure of speech, because nine verses later it says: *"But," He said, "you cannot see my face, for man shall not see me and live," (Exodus 33:20).*

Moses could not tolerate the fullness of the glory of God, lest he die. God is spirit as we have explored, and Moses only saw God's back. Again, it is a figure of speech, meaning Moses saw a degree of his glory. God protected Moses. His deity was too much for man to behold in the flesh.

Earlier in Exodus 3, God encounters Moses through a burning bush. This place of God's presence was revealed through fire — the purifying nature and judgment of death and life. This time, God tells Moses not to come near but to take off his sandals. Sandals and feet were considered to be the dirtiest or unclean parts of the human body. You would take your sandals off and wash your feet before entering someone's house. God was saying: I will speak to you through the fire; I am a consuming fire (Deuteronomy 4:24). Literally his presence is lethal. He deals with sin, uncleanliness, and the filth of this world with fire. Yet on the other hand, God was showing mercy. His presence will not destroy you — it will gently purify you and preserve life. God was showing Moses that the ground he was standing on is holy. Before tabernacling in a tent, God's presence was moving. The moving presence within a bush made the ground holy. It is holy because God is there and holiness is wherever his presence is found.

It was nothing short of amazing that God's consuming presence would dwell with Moses. By now, we are understanding a little more of what it means to be holy, and therefore, what it means to be intimate. It's impossible to commune intimately with God, and not be holy, or set apart, and purified by his presence.

You shall be holy to me, for I the LORD am holy and have separated you from the peoples, that you should be mine. (Leviticus 20:26)

INTIMACY THROUGH HOLINESS

Another way the Bible depicts holiness is through uncommonness. What is common was viewed as unclean or profane. What was uncommon was viewed as holy, reverent and esteemed in awe.

In Genesis 25, Jacob desired his brother Esau's birthright. Scripture says that Esau despised (v. 34) the first born birth rights: his claim to the father's inheritance. The Hebrew word despised means, "treated as common or profane." Esau treated the gift of his father as common, and he gave it up. What was holy and set apart turned into familiarity with God and caused him to overlook his inheritance in favor of feeding his flesh — literally, with a bowl of stew — in a moment of hunger. Jacob went on to birth the Twelve Tribes of Israel, facilitating the lineage of Christ. It was also the function of a priest to teach the nations the statues of the Lord, distinguishing between holy and the common.

You are to distinguish between the holy and the common, and between the unclean and the clean, and you are to teach the people of Israel all the statutes that the LORD has spoken to them by Moses. (Leviticus 10:10–11)

We, too, are a royal priesthood (1 Peter 2:9) and our role remains as such if we are to walk in his presence and teach others to do the same.

When we treat God as common or familiar — in the sense of being like anything else — we profane our inheritance. We miss beholding the glory of God. We become unaccustomed to his presence, and are satisfied with feeding our flesh with an appetite for the world.

Being intimate with God as holy, in awe and wonder, invites us into his inheritance. We know that is realized in Jesus Christ. Commonness in our approach to God will destroy any intimacy God desires. God was showing Moses that he is uncommon, that his name cannot be profaned, and that he cannot be approached casually without first being purified. Intimacy is birthed when we acknowledge our common transgressions — in times when our conscience has felt unclean, guilty, dirty, or polluted through sin — and we draw near to God through Christ. If sin separates and cuts us off from God, like it did to Adam and Eve in the Garden, or Esau and his inheritance, then mercy and forgiveness allow us to draw near. God is always pursuing us with his clean Spirit (Psalm 19:9).

INTIMACY THROUGH FEAR AND AWE

Many times when people came into the presence of God two things occurred. First, they saw the error and filth of their own sin. And second, they experienced an overwhelming sense of dying, fear, or feeling unworthy to be in his presence. Look at John's response:

The hairs of his head were white, like white wool, like snow. His eyes were like a flame of fire, his feet were like burnished bronze, refined in a furnace, and his voice was like the roar of many waters. In his right hand he held seven stars, from his mouth came a sharp two-edged sword, and his face was like the sun shining in full strength.

When I saw him, I fell at his feet as though dead. But he laid his right hand on me, saying, "Fear not, I am the first and the last, and the living one. I died, and behold I am alive forevermore, and I have the keys of Death and Hades." (Revelation 1:14–18)

And Job's encounter with God speaking out a whirlwind:

I had heard of you by the hearing of the ear,
  but now my eye sees you;
therefore I despise myself,
  and repent in dust and ashes. (Job 42:5–6)

Isaiah was in the presence of the Lord and his holiness, and he became undone, recognizing he was unclean.

And the foundations of the thresholds shook at the voice of him who called, and the house was filled with smoke. And I said: "Woe is me! For I am lost; for I am a man of unclean lips, and I dwell in the midst of a people of unclean lips; for my eyes have seen the King, the LORD of hosts!" (Isaiah 6:4–5)

This is why the fear of the Lord is the beginning of all wisdom (Proverbs 1:7). The fear of God was never meant for us to run away from him or to be afraid as Adam hid from God. The fear of the Lord speaks of beholding God with awe and reverence, and wonder at his power and majesty. It helps us see the condition of our sinful lives, and simultaneously, the beauty of his holiness and our need to be washed clean. His wonder invites us in to become like Him. Beholding God with an awe and wonder prevents us from becoming familiar and treating Him as common. It preserves our life from destruction.

> *How you behold God determines the course of your life.*

How we treat his presence determines how intimate or distant we become. The fear of God lived out by dwelling in intimacy will make you wise. You will hear correctly and see clearly what is true.

Often, the disappointment and disillusionment we feel when we think God was not where he should have been, to do what he should have done, in the time that we expected him to do it, can become the divide in our intimacy. This is what occurred with the Israelites at the base of Mount Sinai.

And Moses said to Aaron, "What did this people do to you that you have brought such a great sin upon them?" And Aaron said, "Let not the anger of my lord burn hot. You know the people, that they are set on evil. For they said to me, 'Make us gods who shall go before us. As for this Moses, the man who brought us up out of the land of Egypt, we do not know what has become of him.' So I said to them, 'Let any who have gold take it off.' So they gave it to me, and I threw it into the fire, and out came this calf." (Exodus 32:21–24)

The Israelites became despondent that Moses had disappeared, and perhaps God had taken him. Their hearts had not been purified like Moses. They did not know the intimacy he had experienced with God. Weary and with their hearts still set on evil, they created idols and gods for themselves in the form of a calf or bull. And we see that Aaron tried to shift the blame, reminiscent of the Genesis garden scene. We know earlier, from verse 4, the calf or bull was fashioned carefully. It didn't just happen. They still had the old gods of Egypt in mind. Their sin was intentional, birthed out of a perceived distance from God; that God was not with them. They end up worshiping the created and not the Creator.

Distance from God always creates a distortion of his character, and therefore ours, too.

Moses became angry and smashed the tablets of the Ten Commandments, God's word to his people. He scattered it as powder upon the water and made them drink it (Exodus 32:20–35). It would serve as a reminder of the consequences of the curse of sin's bitterness. We see God's anger at sin, and his wrath against it still lingering with the Israelites. He called them stiff-necked, prideful people, and they were afraid. Yet Moses had relationship with God and negotiated with him. God asked Moses to take the people up out of Egypt into the Promised Land, yet Moses wanted to make something very clear with God. Moses said some of the most profound words found in the Old Testament. He understood that to succeed in anything, especially against foreign armies, that he was not going to do it alone. He had one request.

Now therefore, if I have found favor in your sight, please show me now your ways, that I may know you in order to find favor in your sight. Consider too that this nation is your people." And he said, "My presence will go with you, and I will give you rest." And he said to him, "If your presence will not go with me, do not bring us up from here. For how shall it be known that I have found favor in your sight, I and your people? Is it not in your going with us, so that we are distinct, I and your people, from every other people on the face of the earth?" (Exodus 33:13–16)

Moses understood the key to life was the presence of God. The very thing that distinguished Israel from every other nation was the presence of God — that he was with them. Moses would not take one step in the direction of the Promised Land if God's presence did not go with him. His desire was that he may know God. He didn't ask for a war strategy, map, or plan to get out of Egypt. He didn't ask for provision, resource, or help from a friend. He asked only that God's presence would be with them in the midst of their journey. God's glory, his value, was everything to Moses, and it caused Moses to cry out, "Please show me your glory." He wanted the glorious presence and the value of God to be displayed. (see Exodus 33:18).

Is that the cry of your heart as a disciple? Are you beholding him in all his splendor and power? Are you hanging onto every word he says with awe and wonder? Do you desire to commune and dwell with him, to see him in a new light, to know him, and to experience him intimately? Like Moses, you can, too, if you desire.

INTIMACY THROUGH THE MARRIAGE

Shortly after, God reveals his identity and character (which we explored in Chapter 1) to Moses. His mercy and grace are still upon Israel. For the second time, God called Moses up to the mountain of God, Mount Sinai, to establish the Ten Commandments on two tablets of stone. God is the God of second chances — and third and fourth and fifth chances...

Beholding God's presence is not just about emotional feelings. Feelings should flow from truth. God desires to communicate his words for action. There is a deep relational dynamic where we walk and talk with God our Father, listening to his instructions to multiply his image across the Earth. But he does not share his heart with those who dismiss him or disregard his presence. He will not cast his pearls before swine and have them trampled on (Matthew 7:6). He is to be desired and to be thirsted after if he is to share his covenant secrets with his people (see Deuteronomy 29:29).

The way we view or approach God's Word, the Bible, reveals how we view him. God's Ten Commandments — or Ten Words, as they were known — have often been viewed as a recipe of things that keep you out of trouble, used religiously as a form of punishment if we break them. But that is to reduce God's covenant to mere works. God's word speaks of a much deeper narrative. The heart of the Ten Commandments is love and preserving truth. It was viewed by Moses as a vow between God and his people. Moses' encounter on Sinai is symbolic of a wedding between the bride (us) and the bridegroom (God). The first four commandments speak of our relationship with God, and the last six commandments pertain to our relationship with others. Just before the commands are listed, the Bible says that God is a jealous God (Exodus 20:5). The imagery is a jealous or single-minded lover — a bridegroom. This means that he wants you all to himself. Listen to the language of love in the first four commandments from God to Moses on Mount Sinai:

You shall have no other gods before me.

You shall not make for yourself a carved image, or any likeness of anything that is in heaven above, or that is in the earth beneath, or that is in the water under the earth. You shall not bow down to them or serve them, for I the LORD your God am a jealous God, visiting the iniquity of the fathers on the children to the third and the fourth generation of those who hate me, but showing steadfast love to thousands of those who love me and keep my commandments.

You shall not take the name of the LORD your God in vain, for the LORD will not hold him guiltless who takes his name in vain.

Remember the Sabbath day, to keep it holy. (Exodus 20:3–8)

There is a preparation before the marriage starts in Exodus 19:10. There are instructions for Israel, the bride, to wash her garments to be consecrated to her husband to stand under the canopy of a cloud on the mountain and commit their vows. The Ten Commandments are vows between the God of Israel whom he pursued and chose. With every marriage, there is a contract. In God's case, it is a covenant written on two stones, and later, the Son of God's blood. His Word will stand forever despite what the bride will do.

The covenant's first words declare that no other lover shall come before him and Israel. His love is a jealous love. God does not want to share his bride with any other pagan god in an act of adultery. Like a devoted spouse, God does not want us dwelling on past pagan lovers. We shouldn't have images or pictures of them before our eyes, and we shouldn't create images to worship. God's people are made in his image, so let our love and worship be for him alone. God has also given his people his name: Beloved. Just as a bride would take a husband's name, God has revealed his nature so we could walk in the identity that God has given. He has said not to take his name in vain, and don't treat it as common or profane it. It is holy. Therefore, we represent him, and we are holy too. Finally, God says we are to rest in him. He will comfort us. He will be our Sabbath — a time to rest, remember, reflect, and get to know each other deeply. For this is what we will do forever (Revelation 21)!

The Ten Commandments is the greatest love letter ever written in stone. Jealous love is on display in the form of a wedding on top of God's mountain. The bride and groom are enveloped by a cloud of holy presence, where the exchange of words and promises pertaining to life and love are given. The same God invites you to trust and believe his words are life for you.

The Commandments of God are often called the Ten Words of the Covenant. They represent God's presence and commitment among his people and the means in which we should host his presence in relationship to one another. Moses knew the key to victory was intimacy, the very presence of God abiding with them, just as the psalmist David says:

> *Even though I walk through the valley of the shadow of death,*
> *I will fear no evil,*
> *for you are with me;*
> *your rod and your staff,*
> *they comfort me*
> *You prepare a table before me*
> *in the presence of my enemies;*
> *you anoint my head with oil;*
> *my cup overflows.*
> *Surely goodness and mercy shall follow me*
> *all the days of my life,*
> *and I shall dwell in the house of the LORD*
> *forever. (Psalm 23:4–6)*

"You are with me." Are there no better words to hear about the God we call Father? This is not meant for some of the time or on Sunday's or when we view ourselves as good. No, covenant love is forever, 24/7. Knowing God in this way is crucial for developing intimacy.

Again, we see the rich language of "goodness and mercy" following David, as we have formerly read. "Following," in this description is a passionate chase, not just meandering along behind. Mercy runs after us. It also followed Abraham and Moses and it pursued Israel into the Promised Land. If God is with you, if God is for you, who can be against you? (Romans 8:31). If we, just like Israel was instructed, would humble ourselves and obey him, we can come to know the intimacy of God the Father and we shall "dwell" in his presence forever.

A Christian — a person distinguished by God's presence.

When we reflect on this mountain experience meaning, Sinai is from the Hebrew word *sîn*, pronounced "seen." It means "thorn," or "clay" in Hebrew. The intimacy of God would only be revealed in a greater way. Mount Sinai foreshadows that the greatest display of intimacy would come through a suffering servant, and King Jesus Christ who would wear a crown of thorns for our redemption.

THE MOUNT OF OLIVES

The pathway of presence leads us to the Mount of Olives, in the New Testament, also known for its thorns, where we explore the ultimate love of God found in Jesus Christ.

The temporary dwelling and somewhat distant presence of God in the Old Testament was prophesied to come closer — flesh and blood, walking, talking, and breathing close. The Messiah and Son of God left Heaven, stooped down to the Earth he made, and came to dwell with mankind.

And the Word became flesh and dwelt among us, and we have seen his glory, glory as of the only Son from the Father, full of grace and truth. (John 1:14)

The Word, the voice, the fullness of the divine expression of God in his Son came to dwell intimately among us. Herod summoned his wise men to find this baby called Jesus and destroy him. But when they did, they fell down and worshiped him (Matthew 2:10). They recognized glory! They understood in their hearts the words that Jesus would later speak.

If you had known me, you would have known my Father also. From now on you do know him and have seen him. (John 14:7)

God's promise and word literally came to us in flesh. His word speaks to his power. The world was created through his word: "Let there be light." Jesus was the word. The Greeks defined *logos* (translated "word" in English) as an abstract divine spark, a message or an ordering principle for the world, but John defines *logos* as personal — as the life of all men (John 1:4). John was saying the true person of God has been given to us in Jesus. Behold him, know him, hear him, and experience him. He has come to save and to dwell. He is God.

INTIMACY WITH JESUS

The Tabernacle was always a temporary measure for hosting the presence of God, but he desired to take up residence in the hearts of men and women. The tent was symbolic for a mutual dwelling place that Jesus would later take up residence in our bodies. To do so, he would have to permanently make a way for his Spirit to abide in us. Clean hearts and holy lives would be necessary. He would have to be the sacrifice of blood and the holiness required. Man could not do this or save himself. Jesus was fully God and sinless so that he could save, and he was fully man so that he could take the sins of the world upon his body. This exchange was prepared before the foundation of the world. In the ultimate act of intimacy, Jesus was set to go to the cross to die and lay his life down for us.

But when Christ appeared as a high priest of the good things that have come, then through the greater and more perfect tent (not made with hands, that is, not of this creation) he entered once for all into the holy places, not by means of the blood of goats and calves but by means of his own blood, thus securing an eternal redemption. (Hebrews 9:11–12)

The Romans paraded their own glory and power. Jesus came in obscurity. His glory was veiled. Only one time, on a mountain, did a few of his disciples see him being transfigured in glorious light (Matthew 17:2–3). A glimpse of his divinity was revealed in that moment. Moses reappeared on the scene, speaking, face-to-face again. Jesus' divinity was evidenced. He was the God of Moses and Elijah. The book of Colossians describes perhaps one of the most profound statements about Jesus Christ's deity:

For in him the whole fullness of deity dwells bodily, and you have been filled in him, who is the head of all rule and authority. (Colossians 2:9–10)

The magi saw him as a human baby and beheld his divinity as God. He did not grow into becoming God, he was God. The Son of God and Son of Man would walk the Earth with a mission to seek and save that which was lost (Luke 19:10). In his humanity, he could relate to us and we to him. He could sympathize with us because he knows the pain of humanity's suffering. Because he was a man he knew every trial and temptation we would go through, and it was in his suffering that the greatest display of intimacy took place.

At the foot of the Mount of Olives is a place called Gethsemane, which means "oil press." It is here that Jesus prayed one of the most intimate prayers in much anguish.

Then Jesus went with them to a place called Gethsemane, and he said to his disciples, "Sit here, while I go over there and pray." And taking with him Peter and the two sons of Zebedee, he began to be sorrowful and troubled. Then he said to them, "My soul is very sorrowful, even to death; remain here, and watch with me." And going a little farther he fell on his face and prayed, saying, "My Father, if it be possible, let this cup pass from me; nevertheless, not as I will, but as you will." (Matthew 26:36–39)

For Jesus, suffering didn't start on the cross. Suffering started mentally and emotionally in his soul, knowing he would also physically suffer. The oil press was the place where the olives were crushed with pressing stones. He would feel and know every part of death and its crushing even before breathing His last breath. "Anointing" means "to smear." Jesus Christ, the anointed one — the smeared one, illustrates his anointing as the true King and also how his body would be prepared and anointed for death.

Whether it be the crushing of an olive or the sacrifice of death that a seed will undergo in the soil to display a plant, Jesus displayed this physically by dying on this earth. The actual revelation of his death, was illustrated when he stated:

Truly, truly, I say to you, unless a grain of wheat falls into the earth and dies, it remains alone; but if it dies, it bears much fruit. Whoever loves his life loses it, and whoever hates his life in this world will keep it for eternal life. (John 12:24–25)

Jesus was himself the figurative grain of wheat. Through his life and death, we begin to see how humility produces intimacy, and intimacy leads to life for all. Christ knew His identity and mission in the Father. He surrendered his soul in the Garden of Gethsemane on the Mount of Olives. The fragrance of his obedience was produced in pouring out his heart and will with the words, "Not my will, but yours be done." Christ's intimacy with the Father is the reason we can know the intimacy of Christ. Identity, humility, and intimacy was his pathway.

If we are to abide in Jesus, oil must be present. Without the oil of knowing his suffering, there is no fragrance or life of his resurrection.

INTIMACY THROUGH PRAYER

Jesus had asked the disciples to pray with him three times, and every time, they failed to abide. They are literally and metaphorically asleep to his suffering. However, where the disciples initially missed it, the Apostle Paul would understand the key to intimacy with Jesus years later.

That I may know him and the power of his resurrection, and may share his sufferings, becoming like him in his death. (Philippians 3:10)

To know, to share, to become like — these are the words Paul used, and they are inescapably tied to the death, burial, and resurrection of Jesus.

Often, we confuse our poor choices in life with suffering. That is, we suffer as a result of not following God's word and truth for our circumstances. We suffer from our own disobedience because of straying from the path of presence and truth. That's not what Paul is talking about. Paul is talking about sharing in the suffering of Jesus. There is always grace for this suffering. We share in this type of suffering when we are rejected because of him, are persecuted because we are his children, when we die to things of this world, leave our old ways behind, swallow our pride, or feel the need to justify ourselves because we have been wronged, yet hold our tongue. When we take the unpopular road — the road of the Spirit — we are sharing intimately in the suffering of Christ and becoming like him. There is an intimacy in this type of suffering that no other road produces. The pathway of intimacy will always pass through suffering "like" Jesus, but it promises to be full of joy in his presence. Jesus knew this joy to be true. His joy was pleasing the Father. His joy had us in mind.

Looking to Jesus, the founder and perfecter of our faith, who for the joy that was set before him endured the cross, despising the shame, and is seated at the right hand of the throne of God. (Hebrews 12:2)

For Jesus, the ability to surrender his will in Gethsemane was only possible because the Spirit of God remained upon him. His flesh was crying out for another way to please his Father, but his Spirit was willing to do whatever his Father had in mind. The Holy Spirit allowed Christ to be sustained and tethered to the Father during extreme times of pressing, and he can do the same for us. In Matthew 26:41, it teaches us about Christ's moment in Gethsemane and is a key for our endurance in his presence. It has to do with prayer.

Watch and pray that you may not enter into temptation. The spirit indeed is willing, but the flesh is weak. (Matthew 26:41)

The disciples were sleeping. The temptation wasn't to fall into any obvious expression of sin in the moment. The temptation was to be blinded to the work of the Spirit of God who would conquer death through life in a risen Savior, bringing his Kingdom to Earth. The temptation was to ignore sharing in Jesus' suffering, and therefore, be blinded to the joy of knowing his presence. They would miss the hour of glory (see Matthew 26:45). Jesus was so desperate for them to stay awake so they could abide in him. The story is more than just a matter of physical sleep, it was a spiritual slumbering to the Spirit.

INTIMACY IN ABIDING WITH THE HOLY SPIRIT

If we are to develop intimacy as disciples and learn to dwell in his presence, then we must come to know the person of the Holy Spirit. It is impossible to come to Jesus without the Holy Spirit. The Father draws us to Jesus. If God is Spirit, then it is by his Holy Spirit that we are drawn close.

No one can come to me unless the Father who sent me draws him. And I will raise him up on the last day. (John 6:44)

We cannot even truthfully declare or believe in his name without the Holy Spirit.

Therefore I want you to understand that no one speaking in the Spirit of God ever says "Jesus is accursed!" and no one can say "Jesus is Lord" except in the Holy Spirit. (1 Corinthians 12:3)

Surely then, if we are to get to know Christ, who is now in Heaven, we must know his Holy Spirit who he sent upon the Earth to dwell with mankind. He is the Spirit of God.

If the Spirit of him who raised Jesus from the dead dwells in you, he who raised Christ Jesus from the dead will also give life to your mortal bodies through his Spirit who dwells in you. (Romans 8:11)

The first chapter of Romans teaches us that we can know something about the attributes of God through his creation (Romans 1:20). Intrinsic within the original created world is all that points to God. The Spirit of God permeates in and through what he has spoken to life. He, the person of the Holy Spirit, was not just poured out for the New Testament Church but was present through Christ as the agent of creation in the beginning. The Spirit of God was dwelling with man in the cool of the Garden, hovering and moving — tabernacling, if you like (Genesis 1:2).

Only a few Old Testament figures knew what it was to experience the Spirit of God — at least in a manner that the Spirit of God remained with them for a period of time. The Spirit of God came upon Bezaleel (see Exodus 35:31) for the task of constructing the tabernacle. He came upon Samson (see Judges 14:6) and Othniel (see Judges 3:10) to judge and deliver Israel from their oppressors. He came upon Saul to prophesy (see 1 Sam 11:6). He was even with Joseph to interpret dreams (see Genesis 41:38). As we have discussed, the Israelites' access to God was through a mediator — a priest — and only the High Priest was able to be the closest to the presence of God.

Taking some imaginative liberties, we may one day be able to ask these people what it was like to achieve such great feats. But we might be surprised to hear them ask us, "What was it like to have the permanent indwelling of the Spirit of God within you?" His presence was something Israel only witnessed from a distance or sporadically.

The Spirit of God has made me, and the breath of the Almighty gives me life. (Job 33:4)

Pneuma, (pronounced nyoo'-mah) is the Greek word for "spirit." It's also the word for the movement of air, a wind, or breath. The equivalent Old Testament word is *Ruach* (roo-akh), which is portrayed here in Job's words. Spirit and wind are interchangeable. The imagery presents the Spirit of God as the breath of God, and breath is needed for life. God is pneuma. He is not reduced to wind, but rather, he is the life and breath of all creation. Just like you breathe in and out right now from your respiratory system, he holds the inspiration and expiration to all of your days.

Whether a man or woman believes in God or not, he or she is made in the image of God by the Spirit of God. You are being sustained today, not only by the air that God breathed into your lungs as he did with Adam — a lump of clay fashioned and shaped, filled with the expiration of atoms into flesh — but you are alive because the Spirit of God has made you. We live, move, and exist not just because we were created but because of who created us and personally sustains us. This is the work of the pneuma of God.

To those who believe, he is more than breath, he is personal. And he desires for us to abide and be closer than the air you breathe.

Jesus says:
Abide in me, and I in you. As the branch cannot bear fruit by itself, unless it abides in the vine, neither can you, unless you abide in me. I am the vine; you are the branches. Whoever abides in me and I in him, he it is that bears much fruit, for apart from me you can do nothing. (John 15:4–5)

Branches don't have to struggle to rest in the vine, they simply do.

We have been grafted into the tree of life through Jesus. Every nutrient and good thing that reaches the branches comes from his life. We are fed through Jesus when we have taken up our abode in him. When our minds are dwelling on him and his words. He is the support system, and without his strength and power, we can do nothing that bears real fruit.

This is what Jesus said would occur after he was raised from dead:

Nevertheless, I tell you the truth: it is to your advantage that I go away, for if I do not go away, the Helper will not come to you. But if I go, I will send him to you. (John 16:7)

How can it be better? If Jesus goes away, it can be better only because now his Spirit will be poured out on all flesh permanently, not just a select few who are in his presence on Earth. Every male and female can know what it is to have the Spirit of God abiding in them permanently. He is the helper, and he helps us remember who Jesus is, what he said, and how we should live and dwell accordingly.

When the Spirit of truth comes, he will guide you into all the truth, for he will not speak on his own authority, but whatever he hears he will speak, and he will declare to you the things that are to come. He will glorify me, for he will take what is mine and declare it to you. All that the Father has is mine; therefore I said that he will take what is mine and declare it to you. (John 16:13–15)

Abiding takes sensitivity. The Holy Spirit will develop an intimacy when we are careful to hear his voice and obey. He wants us to know him as a sheep knows the shepherd's voice — with hours, days, and months listening to the directions and calling of the shepherd. Jesus says he is our good shepherd in John 10:14. His voice will often be a still, quiet voice. It will leap with the life of his desire, not always yours, and it will be confirmed as being in accordance with the truth of the Bible.

How do you abide? Just as in any relationship, there is no substitute for time — time spent getting to know his character, his ways, and his mission for our life. His voice will become distinguishable when we spend time with him and his word. Just like a little child just naturally hears their mother or father, so, too, we can hear the voice of the Holy Spirit. You don't have to teach a child to hear, there is no manual for that, they simply hear by being in close proximity over time — and predominantly to his word.

We abide by listening, obeying, and digesting his word which guides and leads us in truth. We can talk, worship, praise, pray, pour out our hearts, become vulnerable, grieve, share our thoughts, give him our fears, reconcile with others, dwell on his character and beauty, and let his Spirit conform us to his will.

We truly abide when we are led not by our own desires but by a desire to be in his presence and please his will.

Remember, the old you got crucified. We are following his lead. This was the dynamic that took place in Gethsemane. Such was the intimacy of Jesus with the Father, that he did not want to do anything that would displease his will. We can know this type of intimacy if we see the personhood of the Holy Spirit.

He is referred to as Holy Spirit. When we entertain anything unclean — or as we have discussed, "common" — his presence cannot abide in us. We must turn again to him, obey his command to be set apart, and acknowledge that there are things that grieve him and things that please him. Because he is personal, it is possible for him to be grieved by our choices and unholy ways. If we are walking in intimacy we should know when we have fallen short and ask for forgiveness.

And do not grieve the Holy Spirit of God, by whom you were sealed for the day of redemption. Let all bitterness and wrath and anger and clamor and slander be put away from you, along with all malice. Be kind to one another, tenderhearted, forgiving one another, as God in Christ forgave you. (Ephesians 4:30–32)

We have been justified by the work and person of Jesus Christ, yet proof of his dwelling and transforming work in our hearts and minds is obedience to the sanctifying work of his Holy Spirit. The abiding life always results in transformation. It results in bearing good fruit — fruit of the Spirit.

But the fruit of the Spirit is love, joy, peace, patience, kindness, goodness, faithfulness, gentleness, self-control; against such things there is no law. And those who belong to Christ Jesus have crucified the flesh with its passions and desires.

If we live by the Spirit, let us also keep in step with the Spirit. (Galatians 5:22–25)

Just as the branches abide in the vine, our lives don't have to strive to produce love, joy, or peace, but a keen consciousness that he is with us allows us to ask the question, "What do you want, Holy Spirit?" This is how we keep in step with his voice and truth, and this is how he helps us, if we desire it. Read these verses carefully on the Holy Spirit.

To dwell with him is to be continually regenerated into new life:
Therefore, if anyone is in Christ, he is a new creation. The old has passed away; behold, the new has come. (2 Corinthians 5:17)

To dwell with him is to be accepted and known:
The Spirit himself bears witness with our spirit that we are children of God, and if children, then heirs — heirs of God and fellow heirs with Christ, provided we suffer with him in order that we may also be glorified with him. (Romans 8:16–17)

To dwell with him is to be sealed with a promise in Christ as our inheritance:
In him you also, when you heard the word of truth, the gospel of your salvation, and believed in him, were sealed with the promised Holy Spirit, who is the guarantee of our inheritance until we acquire possession of it, to the praise of his glory. (Ephesians 1:13–14)

To dwell with him is to be adopted into God's family and delivered from fear:
For you did not receive the spirit of slavery to fall back into fear, but you have received the Spirit of adoption as sons, by whom we cry, "Abba! Father!" (Romans 8:15)

To dwell with him is to become holy like him:
But we ought always to give thanks to God for you, brothers beloved by the Lord, because God chose you as the firstfruits to be saved, through sanctification by the Spirit and belief in the truth. (2 Thessalonians 2:13)

To dwell with him is to be able to do great things for him:
For we are his workmanship, created in Christ Jesus for good works, which God prepared beforehand, that we should walk in

them. (Ephesians 2:10)

INTIMACY IN ABIDING IN THE WORD

If you walk in the pathway of his presence, you will no doubt be faced with his words of love and instruction. The word of God is a lamp unto our feet, a light unto our path (Psalm 119:105). Assuming you are this far along the path of presence and discipleship, Bible reading is already a non-negotiable, yet many don't see the word as living and active for the "now." Much could be said about the presence of his word in our life. Active transformation through dwelling on the scriptures, conforming us day by day to be like Jesus, needs to be our posture. It is important to see the word of God in its correct light — alive, otherwise reading the Bible will become a chore or simply good history lessons.

The Bible is 66 books, composed supernaturally over 1,400 years, comprising over 300 prophecies about Jesus the Messiah's coming. The Bible, in its common denominator, points to the main character, Jesus Christ. To read the Bible is to read the story of Christ's redemption and fulfillment of the promises of God — that he may dwell with us. The Bible in its true context with all its individual books divinely orchestrated together, whether it be a letter, poem, law of instructions, books of wisdom, prophetic messages, or historical accounts of individuals, in its culmination — it is revealing the glory of Jesus Christ.

Jesus said to the Jewish religious elite in *John 5:39–40:*

You search the Scriptures because you think that in them you have eternal life; and it is they that bear witness about me, yet you refuse to come to me that you may have life.

Words on the pages of our Bible have life only because they bear witness to Jesus Christ, not because they are written with ink like any other piece of literature. He was the word in flesh. They are living words (Hebrews 4:12), breathed upon by his Holy Spirit, and they speak of him from Genesis to Revelation.

God's presence involves his spoken word. He wants to share his life-giving words and have them reside in your mind and heart permanently.

As disciples of presence we are to hunger and thirst for his word. Read it like a wide-eyed young child, following the simplistic thread of hope. Study his ways like a diligent student, recognizing the good news that Jesus has come as the hero of the story, and he has overcome.

For this reason, many who start their journey of discipleship first read the Gospels — Matthew, Mark, Luke, and John — to understand who Jesus is and what he has done for us. Or perhaps you have begun with a letter like Ephesians in the New Testament, written by the Apostle Paul, explaining our identity in Christ and how to walk with him. By now, hopefully you're also seeing that even the Old Testament, which makes up nearly two thirds of the Bible, reveals the richness of God's heart for his people and the context in which Jesus came to fulfill the Trinity's plan of redemption. The value of Jesus is very much concealed in the Old Testament and expressed clearly in the New Testament.

Bible reading is more than memorizing scriptures, completing reading plans, or mentally acquiring knowledge of historical accounts. Bible reading should be viewed as a way of encountering the word who is Jesus, allowing his words to fill our minds and spirit, so that we might grow in intimacy with him. It is his story in you and you in his story.

So faith comes from hearing, and hearing through the word of Christ. (Romans 10:17)

The majority of biblical communities of antiquity did not have access to reading the scrolls of the Bible. The only way they could know the words of God for their life was to hear them, to have some priestly representation speak them out for the congregation to listen and remember. We are blessed with many options in a world of technology to digest and read the words of Christ, including commentaries and concordances that help us understand what the author intended for us to see. Yet we also have the power of the Holy Spirit to help us. We grow in our faith and intimacy with God only through hearing, reading, listening, and seeing the word of Christ. The motive for our Bible reading should not be a chore — the motive is to know him! To let him read you. The motive is to commune in his presence.

When heard with the ears of the spirit, the word of God becomes the fertile ground for intimacy.

As disciples, intimacy only develops when the word is hidden in our hearts (Psalm 119:11). That's where the word needs to dwell — in our hearts, not just our heads. It — or should we say he — was designed to transform you, not just inform you. This makes sense when we view the word of God as invitational not just prescriptive.

Being tethered to the presence of God will not just tickle your ears, it will challenge you. It will offend your flesh or carnal man. It will continually correct and lead you into the fulfillment of joy and truth — Jesus. This is what the living Scriptures can do in us:

All Scripture is breathed out by God and profitable for teaching, for reproof, for correction, and for training in righteousness, that the man of God may be complete, equipped for every good work. (2 Timothy 3:16–17)

When the word of God is hidden in our heart with intimacy, when there is a desire to know him and his presence through studying his word, it will begin to equip and train you for everything in life! (More on this in the next chapter!)

THE INTIMACY OF WORSHIPING JESUS

Like the spirit or soul of a human, wind and breath speak of that which is immaterial. Jesus says to the Samaritan woman at the well that the worship of God must not be reduced to the material location. There was contention between people about the true place of worship — Jerusalem for the Jews and Mount Gerizim for the Samaritans (John 4). But Spirit-led worship is expressed in the immaterial — the heart, emotion, desire, and will. It is led by truth — the knowledge of God and his word in Christ Jesus.

So, whether you eat or drink, or whatever you do, do all to the glory of God. (1 Corinthians 10:31)

Worship cannot be confined to a church service or even a song. The worship God desires is anywhere, at any time, in all that you think and do. It is a constant inner praise expressed in our service to him.

Intimacy is nurtured when we worship, because worship is remembering the goodness of God.

All the ends of the earth shall remember
  and turn to the LORD,
and all the families of the nations
  shall worship before you. (Psalm 22:27)

God has given us his Spirit so that we might remember him and worship him. Such was the anguish he felt in Gethsemane, that Jesus would exhale his last breath on the cross and give up his Spirit so that we could exhale his praises today.

On the last day of the feast, the great day, Jesus stood up and cried out, "If anyone thirsts, let him come to me and drink. Whoever believes in me, as the Scripture has said, 'Out of his heart will flow rivers of living water.'" Now this he said about the Spirit, whom those who believed in him were to receive, for as yet the Spirit had not been given, because Jesus was not yet glorified. (John 7:37–39)

Jesus speaks of his Spirit as waters that flow like rivers. He chooses the setting of the Feast of Tabernacles — meaning "dwelling" — to announce the most striking of truths. The temple courts were overflowing with thousands of people worshiping and waving their fall harvest offerings to God, thanking him for their crops they just reaped, and asking for rain for the new harvest. Thanksgiving is always at the heart of worship.

A water pouring ceremony held by the priests was led by the people's desperate cries of Hosanna, "O Lord, save us!" (Psalm 118:25), which also pertains to their physical survival: Save us by sending rain.

On the seventh day of the feast, Jesus waits for a moment of quiet in the ceremony and bellows out the revelation that he is the waters — the ultimate answer to their survival and the reason for their worship. He is their thirst-quencher, and many failed to behold his presence among them. While the priests drew from the springs of water from the Earth, only the Spirit of Jesus can bring true, refreshing, and saving life. What a bold statement that would have been. Jesus essentially said that all of what you celebrate and cry out for is really him. He is the fulfillment of the feast — a tabernacling God — who offers river-flowing life.

To be thirsty for him is to worship him and thank him for his Spirit in you. When we behold Jesus as the source of our life, we say, "Here I am. Have all of me." Beholding Jesus is more than casually approaching him with a song. It speaks of an intention, grip, or fixation. To behold the beauty of his holiness in worship means that he has all of your undivided attention and efforts. Worship becomes a lifestyle when we are mindful of his presence in all that we do, and as we will explore, worship is also a weapon against the enemy.

INTIMACY THROUGH PRAYER AND FASTING

Intimacy is fashioned in the furnace of prayer and fasting. There is much to say about prayer and fasting, but first let us just look at the heart of prayer. The following chapters will discuss the role of prayer.

As we have read, Jesus' most intimate moment is found in the Garden of Gethsemane in the form of a cry of prayer. Prayer, in its basic form, is honest conversation with God. Anybody can do this! Jesus had already taught the disciples how to pray and he examples this highlighted by the initial words "My Father" on the Mount of Olives. It's the prayer of selflessness. It's a prayer for us to be led by God and not be the sole focus. It's a prayer to be delivered from evil and to keep in step with the Spirit so that we can glorify him. The key to Jesus' ministry was his time in prayer to the Father. He often went away from the crowds and withdrew to a quiet place to hear the words and directions of his Father. He was constantly conforming to the Father's will amidst the noise of the world. We become like Jesus when we conform to the thoughts and prayers of Jesus. Our prayers are only heard by God because they are prayed through Christ.

Jesus illustrated the prototype of prayer the disciples should pray earlier on in his ministry:

Pray then like this:

> *Our Father in heaven,*
>   *hallowed be your name.*
> *Your kingdom come,*
>   *your will be done,*
> *on earth as it is in heaven.*
>   *Give us this day our daily bread,*
> *and forgive us our debts,*
>   *as we also have forgiven our debtors.*

> *And lead us not into temptation,*
>   *but deliver us from evil. (Matthew 6:9–13)*

"Our Father" — the language is intimate. As a son and daughter of God, we can call him not just Father but "my Father." Jesus is first exalting the Father and the nature of his name. Prayer is to be poured out, communing in his attributes. If you do not know what to pray, just start by telling him who he is. In doing so, the presence of God will surround your heart and mind, revealing who you are. Again, this reiterates our first mountain of his identity as being crucial for prayer.

Prayer recognizes daily bread as the word of God that sustains us. We don't just live off physical food but we live by every word that comes from his mouth (Matthew 4:4). It gives us the ability to avoid evil and walk in righteousness. This type of prayer allows the rule and reign of Christ to take place in our minds, families, jobs, and daily routines.

There is a heart of dependence in this type of praying. God knows we have all kinds of needs and requests. He knows them before we ask (Matthew 6:8). We can approach him as Father in faith that when we pray according to his will, our prayers are heard and are cared for.

> *And this is the confidence that we have toward him, that if we ask anything according to his will he hears us. (1 John 5:14)*

Prayers of intimacy are much more than presenting a shopping list of what we want before God. Prayers exchange the depths of our heart for the depths of his. The Holy Spirit will help us with how to pray his will. That's why it's important to know his character.

The Apostle Paul tell us Jesus is peace, and he connects the concept of not worrying to the power of prayer:

The Lord is at hand; do not be anxious about anything, but in everything by prayer and supplication with thanksgiving let your requests be made known to God. And the peace of God, which surpasses all understanding, will guard your hearts and your minds in Christ Jesus. (Philippians 4:5b–7)

Submit everything in prayer? That is significant. When we are at peace in prayer, we have intimacy with God. His assurance is present through his Spirit guarding our minds and heart.

Jesus felt the anxiousness and the pain of the cross so that we could rest in his peace.

We pray from the completed work that Jesus has already done on the cross. We pray from the place of being intimate sons and daughters, not begging but able to approach our Father with boldness (Hebrews 4:16), as forgiven and clean in Jesus.

We pray the promises of his words, not just our words. We pray the scriptures back to God, laying hold of what he has said to be true. We pray his will, not ours. When we conform to the image of Christ, we know what his will is and we become less self-focused and more focused on the Kingdom of God.

And when you fast, do not look gloomy like the hypocrites, for they disfigure their faces that their fasting may be seen by others. Truly, I say to you, they have received their reward. (Matthew 6:17)

Jesus said "when you fast" because he expected fasting to be a natural part of our life as followers of him. He expected that it would be done in the secret place, without us boasting about it. Fasting means going without food. It's not talked about much today. We would rather take delight in speaking about amazing food. Yet the scriptures clearly show us the power of denying our flesh in the form of the pleasure of food. When we go without food for periods of times, we are withholding something physical in order to draw closer to the things of the Spirit. Fasting without praying is just starving ourselves. But when we pray and fast, we are able to clearly hear what the Holy Spirit wants from us. Fasting develops a greater environment in our hearts that is conducive to communing, dwelling, and being sensitive to hear his voice.

The disciples once asked Jesus why they could not cast out evil spirits from a young boy, and he replied:

"This kind can come out by nothing but prayer and fasting." (Mark 9:29, NKJV)

While not all translations will include the word fasting in the above passage, there is a spiritual intensity and intimacy developed about our prayer life when we go without food for a period of time. There is less distraction from the world's desires and as we see, there is access to his power to see miracles, signs, and wonders when we pray and fast. Prayer opens the door for God to do what seems impossible. This is because we begin to see what is taking place in the spirit when we pray. We can pray from the place of intimacy, knowing the One who we are praying too. Our prayers can be full of faith, not distant or formula-based, but according to his will, his word, and his heart. There is a deeper place of dwelling that God is inviting us to by his Holy Spirit, a place of his Spirit that has access to Heaven's perspective for Earth. When we humble ourselves, we can truly seek his face, and he can heal our hearts and nation. *If my people who are called by my name humble themselves, and pray and seek my face and turn from their wicked ways, then I will hear from heaven and will forgive their sin and heal their land. (2 Chronicles 7:14)*

Prayer was designed for us to know him and to understand what he does with it. As we will see next, it is a weapon against Satan for those who believe.

SUMMARY

The biblical encounters with God at Mount Sinai and the Mount of Olives teach us the means and purpose of our existence in intimately dwelling with him. Intimacy is developed when we follow the pattern of humility. Laying down our lives enables the Holy Spirit to enter our hearts and develop a relationship with us. Moses understood that the success of his life was due to the presence of God — something he was not willing to go without. He held fast to God's glory, seeking his face, and teaching God's covenant vows to his bride, the people of Israel. In doing so, intimacy was created through obedience to his word, showing us the adventure and boundaries to holy living. We, as a royal priesthood, are to determine by his Spirit and word what is clean and unclean, what is common and what is holy. Through our dwelling with Jesus, people are able to see the Father's goodness and know him, too. Intimacy corrects, challenges, and crucifies the flesh so that we can know the life of Christ and have him inhabit our soul.

Jesus ultimately displays the greatest act of intimacy on the cross. Shortly before that, in the Garden of Gethsemane, Jesus was pouring out his heart to the Father and simultaneously surrendering his will. Jesus depended on the Holy Spirit for his sustaining strength and leading presence. He showed us that true intimacy is found in sharing in his suffering to become like him.

Through abiding in the Holy Spirit poured out for us, we can commune in God's word, pray his perfect will, and worship his holy name in all that we do. Glory is given to God through our lives only from the place of cultivating intimacy.

AUTHORITY

Mount Carmel to the Mount of Temptation

Empowered living in Christ.

Authority is a misunderstood and misrepresented word in today's society. For many, it often conjures up images of abuse, corruption, misguided strength, and selfish preservation of power and wealth. The Kingdom of God however defines authority much differently. Authority in the Kingdom is given to serve those around us, not control them. Authority in the Kingdom doesn't fight for power and position but preserves and protects. *Authority in the Kingdom is given to us by Jesus to overcome the works of the enemy and to witness his good works here on earth so that others may know him.* Many Christians are oblivious to the reality that they even have authority to overcome in this life. As we continue to walk the pathway of his presence as a disciple, we will observe that the three previous mountains of identity, humility, and intimacy pertain mostly to a posture of "being." Our "being" in him never stops; it is essential we live from this place before we get into the "doing," lest our "doing" be in vain. Authority is where the "doing" comes in appropriately.

The root of the word authority is "author." It is only when we have come to intimately know the Author of our life that we can know the authority we have been given by him to overcome sin and its effects.

To know your authority is to know the original author of it.

As we dwell in his presence, we will understand that God will lead us into the work he has created for us. Work is not sin. The laboring and exhaustion of work was the curse of sin that occurred in the Garden of Eden (Genesis 3:19). In other words, work that leads to futile efforts was never part of God's ideal for us. Sin led to futility.

It weakened and destroyed our authority over the Earth when we disobeyed God. We were created to rule and reign with him. Just as we have read, we were designed to have dominion over the Earth.

Then God said, "Let us make man in our image, after our likeness. And let them have dominion over the fish of the sea and over the birds of the heavens and over the livestock and over all the earth and over every creeping thing that creeps on the earth." (Genesis 1:26)

God had created us as his image bearers to rule and reign, but Man abdicated his authority through disobedience, consequently handing over authority to Satan. 2 Corinthians 4:4 even calls him the "god of this world," referring to his temporary earthly authority, as result of humanity's fall. Ever since this time, Man has been in a battle with Satan. He deceived mankind in the Garden of Eden into eating the fruit of the Tree of the Knowledge of Good and Evil. The reality of our distance from God was the evil made known to us.

Before there was a physical battle between humans, there was a spiritual fight in Heaven — a contention for glory. Satan was previously a guardian cherub, an angelic creature of the highest order. In his pride and in his desire to become God rather than worship God, he was thrown out of Heaven (Isaiah 14:12-14) and his fate will one day be eternity in the Lake of Fire (Revelation 20:10).

We know in Genesis, though, that in the meantime, Satan took the form of a serpent and deceived mankind in the Garden. The consequence was a perpetual animosity between humanity and Satan. God said to Satan:

I will put enmity between you and the woman,

> *and between your offspring and her offspring;*
> *he shall bruise your head,*
> *and you shall bruise his heel. (Genesis 3:15)*

This is the battle we know. The "he" is Jesus, who would come through the offspring of man to crush the head of Satan. God displayed his authority over Satan and sin on the cross where death — the consequence of sin — was overcome. God gave Jesus all authority, which Jesus then in turn gave to us to reinstate God's plan in Eden: to have dominion over the Earth and the prince of power of the Earth.

Prolepsis is a fancy word that essentially means "already but not yet." In reference to Jesus Christ, it means that the final and complete work has already been done on the cross. Death has been defeated, conquered in the resurrection by the power of God. Yet, we still see the effects of sin, suffering, and death around us. God already won the ultimate battle, but the time for Jesus to return to Earth again (Titus 2:12 and John 14:3) is "not yet." It is then we shall see him (1 John 3:3) and be present with him. He shall establish the fullness of the expression of the Kingdom of God, which had already come to Earth as Christ as its King (Matthew 3:2). Until then, Satan still has a limited time to rob, kill, and destroy as many people as he can.

The thief comes only to steal and kill and destroy. I came that they may have life and have it abundantly. (John 10:10)

Satan, the accuser of the brethren, has a mission to blind humanity from seeing the image and glory of Jesus and to lead them to a lost eternity separate from God, a place called hell (everlasting torment and punishment). Hell is a destination for angels and humans who reject God.

Then he will say to those on his left, "Depart from me, you cursed, into the eternal fire prepared for the devil and his angels." (Matthew 25:41)

God has no delight in the death of anyone (Ezekiel 18:32). That is why Jesus came to save us.

Christ has come to give life. He has taken back the authority we lost and reinstated our rightful position in him and with him. If intimacy with him has shown us anything, it is that we have been given his identity through the Holy Spirit to know true life.

Just as Adam was called to co-labor with God in the Garden, to name the animals and declare who they were according to their function and nature, our reinstated authority gives us the ability to declare the name of Jesus over our lives and the path we walk on this earth.

No longer under the rule of Satan, we are found in Christ to rule and reign with him. This begins now. You don't have to wait until you are in Heaven; Heaven has come down. Our battle is not with each other, but that is what Satan loves us to think.

The Apostle Paul states it clearly: If you haven't realized yet, you are in a spiritual battle.

For we do not wrestle against flesh and blood, but against the rulers, against the authorities, against the cosmic powers over this present darkness, against the spiritual forces of evil in the heavenly places. (Ephesians 6:12)

Our lives are in a fight whether we acknowledge it or not, but it's a fight of the cosmic order. The quicker we understand the spiritual reality to our existence, the quicker we can be prepared for battle. The reality is the enemy — Satan — is powerful and deceptive. We, as humans in our own strength, are no match for spiritual beings and ranks of armies of darkness. The Eastern world is well aware of the nature of spirits. The Western world often lives in ignorance that they exist and is too occupied by the materialistic or the physical realm.

> *The only reason you can fight a spiritual battle is because God's power fights it for you.*

We fight against the powers of darkness from the position of Christ's great power and "already" position of victory. Why do we need authority? For the times of the "not yet" — the limited time Satan has on this Earth. Authority is required to preach the gospel in the face of persecution and overcome all kinds of evil, temptation, fear, anxiety, sickness, and every demonic spirit desiring to destroy us. Your life and the people you are called to influence with the Gospel need to know the overcoming power of Jesus over Satan and death. This requires that you be keenly aware of the authority you have as a disciple of Christ. This is not your own authority or earthly power we are talking about. This is a spiritual fight that requires spiritual authority. God's presence is full of the true authority in Jesus for you to walk in.

Someone who understood his God-backed authority in the Old Testament was Elijah the prophet — and he was famous for walking in this authority! Elijah lived during one of the most dark, spiritually oppressive times in history which is why his confidence in

God, and security in his God-given authority had people in the New Testament — hundreds of years later — still talking about him. A pinnacle moment in his story took place on a mountaintop where God met him in full power and authority in front of the entire nation.

MOUNT CARMEL

Elijah was one of the few people following God at this time. The majority religion at the time under King Ahab was Baal worship. Baal means "lord" and Mount Carmel means "garden land." So here we have Elijah headed back to the garden land for a showdown between the lord of the land and the Lord God of Israel whom Elijah intimately knew.

The prophets of Baal and King Ahab meet Elijah on Mount Carmel where Elijah challenges them:

Now therefore send and gather all Israel to me at Mount Carmel, and the 450 prophets of Baal and the 400 prophets of Asherah, who eat at Jezebel's table.

So Ahab sent to all the people of Israel and gathered the prophets together at Mount Carmel. And Elijah came near to all the people and said, "How long will you go limping between two different opinions? If the LORD is God, follow him; but if Baal, then follow him." And the people did not answer him a word. Then Elijah said to the people, "I, even I only, am left a prophet of the LORD, but Baal's prophets are 450 men. Let two bulls be given to us, and let them choose one bull for themselves and cut it in pieces and lay it on the wood, but put no fire to it. And I will prepare the other bull and lay it on the wood and put no fire to it. And you call upon the name of your god, and I will call upon the name of the LORD, and the God who answers by fire, he is God." And all the people answered, "It is well spoken." (1 Kings 18:19–24)

The prophets of Baal build their altar, chanting and dancing — even cutting themselves — in a display to call down in authority the power of their god. Elijah is so confident in the power of God that he taunts his enemies, suggesting that Baal must be asleep or busy. The chanting gets louder and the dancing gets wilder, but no fire sparks. It is clear not all gods or deities are the same.

And as midday passed, they raved on until the time of the offering of the oblation, but there was no voice. No one answered; no one paid attention. (1 Kings 18:29)

Now Elijah takes center stage, confident in his authority, born out of years of growing in his identity and intimacy with God, to command this fire. Elijah even pours water on his offering to make a show of the coming glory of God.

Where the presence of God is, there you will find great power and empowering.

Then the fire of the LORD fell and consumed the burnt offering and the wood and the stones and the dust, and licked up the water that was in the trench. And when all the people saw it, they fell on their faces and said, "The LORD, he is God; the LORD, he is God." And Elijah said to them, "Seize the prophets of Baal; let not one of them escape." And they seized them. And Elijah brought them down to the brook Kishon and slaughtered them there. (1 Kings 18:38–40)

Elijah knew his authority in the presence of God, and not only did God show up on full display at Mount Carmel through the fire, but solidified his singularity as Elijah defeated 850 prophets of Baal. Following the fire from the sky, God released the land from its three year drought through Elijah's call and it finally began to rain. How did Elijah know God would show up? Where did Elijah get this authority — beyond confidence or audacity — a true authority to partner with God and overcome actual evil. This kind of authority only comes from intimacy with God, born from humility as a result of an established identity. Elijah had been living the path of presence.

The story takes an odd turn then. Queen Jezebel puts a bounty on his head. And on the heels of making one of the most incomprehensible stands against the powers of the Earth, then witnessing one of the greatest demonstrations of God's power in human history, Elijah runs for his life.

Then he was afraid, and he arose and ran for his life and came to Beersheba, which belongs to Judah, and left his servant there. (1 Kings 19:3)

Elijah went from taunting the physical and spiritual authorities of the land and calling fire from the sky to wanting to die. What caused such a radical turn of events? We must understand that the battle for Elijah, as it is for us, is not a physical battle but a battle for our soul and spirit.

Elijah knew the authority he had because he knew the God who it came from. We see the power of the presence through the fire on the mountaintop. But Elijah isn't on the mountaintop anymore.

Is there more to this authority gained in the presence than just the fire power?

We know that Satan is the accuser and he uses Jezebel to bring accusations against Elijah causing him to question his authority. Jezebel represents a demonic power to kill. Spiritual fear is irrational. It aims to manipulate and control the mind. It promotes hopelessness and a belief that we are unable to be saved from our circumstances. It causes one to withdraw, be passive, lose sight of what image we are created in. It literally drained the energy and will to live out of Elijah.

We need to recognize the enemy's schemes. The spirit of the accuser represented in Ahab and Jezebel aims to deplete our faith and question our authority, causing us to be either controlling or passive and to hold ungodly beliefs about Jesus and ourselves. This type of spirit preys on hurt and offense, stirring bitterness and unforgiveness, leading to rebellion against God — what the Bible calls witchcraft. This spirit feeds off of self-pity and self-seeking attitudes and ultimately desires for us to live ignorant of the authority found in the presence of God.

Accusations from Satan are always loaded with amplified lies that hold no substance when you are in Christ.

This is the clouded perspective that affects Elijah's state of mind following the showdown at Mount Carmel. He even believed that he was the "only one" standing for God, yet God had preserved 7000 others (1 Kings 19:18). Have you ever felt like this? How do we — and how does Elijah — get back to the place of living in authority? First, he needed comforting as we all do in times of exhaustion. An angel brought him food and drink in the desert just as God had done with Moses and Israel (1 Kings 19:7). Then, he strangely travels further away, going back to the mountain of God, Mount Sinai, the mountain of intimacy with God that Moses had experienced.

This is what God says to Elijah:

And he said, "Go out and stand on the mount before the LORD." And behold, the LORD passed by, and a great and strong wind tore the mountains and broke in pieces the rocks before the LORD, but the LORD was not in the wind. And after the wind an earthquake, but the LORD was not in the earthquake. And after the earthquake a fire, but the LORD was not in the fire. And after the fire the sound of a low whisper. And when Elijah heard it, he wrapped his face in his cloak and went out and stood at the entrance of the cave. And behold, there came a voice to him and said, "What are you doing here, Elijah?" (1 Kings 19:11–13)

God was not found in any of the elements like the showdown on Mount Carmel. This time, the authority of God was revealed to Elijah in a whisper or "stillness" or "calm" in the Hebrew language. A whisper is intimate and personal, conveying God's close presence. The authority we walk in because of the presence of God is not just a powerful demonstration — though it can be! But it has staying power beyond the demonstration of power because it is sustained by the intimacy of his presence. God meets us in our dark caves of life — even what to us feels like the grave. If he is the God of Light, he is also sovereign over the darkness. He is familiar with overcoming graves! It is here that Elijah hears the gentle blowing of the voice of God. He is the God who speaks in the silence, to the silence — the darkness. He is ever close in the dark night of our soul. Listen to the life-giving sound of your Creator, he is speaking to you with an inner voice of his Holy Spirit to comfort you and to re-establish you.

Elijah isn't the only one to give us an example of what it looks like to walk in our authority. Jesus himself is the greatest example of understanding the access to our God-given authority born from the path of presence. For he, too, was comforted by the Father's voice when his soul was troubled.

"Now is my soul troubled. And what shall I say? 'Father, save me from this hour'? But for this purpose I have come to this hour. Father, glorify your name." Then a voice came from heaven: "I have glorified it, and I will glorify it again." (John 12:27–28)

We read an incredible story on another mountaintop in the book of Matthew following Jesus' Holy Spirit and water baptism by John the Baptist. Intimacy with the Father has been visibly established and now Jesus turns his attention to the desert at the Mount of Temptation where intimacy gives birth to authority.

THE MOUNT OF TEMPTATION

This leads us to the Mountain of Temptation, the place where Jesus Christ overcame Satan's propositions. We will see there is One whose word is stronger!

If we are to overcome the accusatory words of the enemy, like Elijah heard from Jezebel — words such as, "you're a failure," "your situation is hopeless," "you'll never succeed," "how could you have done that," "you're a fake," "you're guilty, "you're fearful," "what's the point of living," "you're unlovable," — then you will need a more authoritative word.

If you want to fight an argument in the court of law, then you will need a more convincing argument — a truthful argument. In the battle of the spirit, we use THE WORD to fight words. We use the truth of Jesus and his word to overcome lies. Satan is known as the father of all lies (John 8:44). We, as disciples, don't look to our past. That argument finds us guilty, and that is why we cannot fight the enemy by ourselves. Mustering up your own willpower and positive thinking won't win out in a spiritual fight. We must look to our position in Christ. His word over us triumphs over any accusation of the enemy because the accounts of our old sinful nature are paid for by the blood of Jesus.

And they have conquered him by the blood of the Lamb and by the word of their testimony, for they loved not their lives even unto death. (Revelation 12:11)

Authority is given by God and is at work when temptation has tried its best and failed to overcome.

AUTHORITY OVER ACCUSATION AND DECEPTION

The devil comes to tempt, deceive, and accuse us. If we are to overcome the enemy, we must pass through his trappings. The authority of God is used against him in the form of a stronger word. Listen to the approach of Jesus:

Then Jesus was led up by the Spirit into the wilderness to be tempt-

ed by the devil. And after fasting forty days and forty nights, he was hungry. And the tempter came and said to him, "If you are the Son of God, command these stones to become loaves of bread." But he answered, "It is written,

> *"'Man shall not live by bread alone,
> but by every word that comes from the mouth of God.'"*

Then the devil took him to the holy city and set him on the pinnacle of the temple and said to him, "If you are the Son of God, throw yourself down, for it is written,

> *"'He will command his angels concerning you,' and "'On their hands they will bear you up,
> lest you strike your foot against a stone.'"*

Jesus said to him, "Again it is written, 'You shall not put the Lord your God to the test.'" Again, the devil took him to a very high mountain and showed him all the kingdoms of the world and their glory. And he said to him, "All these I will give you, if you will fall down and worship me." Then Jesus said to him, "Be gone, Satan! For it is written,

> *"'You shall worship the Lord your God
> and him only shall you serve.'"*

Then the devil left him, and behold, angels came and were ministering to him. (Matthew 4:1–11)

With every attempt to deceive Jesus into being anything less than he already is, Jesus counteracted the temptation to take an offer of this world with the statement, "It is written" — referring to the scriptures of God in the Old Testament. The devil wanted the worship of Jesus, yet Jesus didn't succumb like Adam and Eve. Instead, he called upon the strength and word of his Father. Jesus could have chosen to remove Satan from the scene, but he chose to appeal to his Father's words that had already been spoken as an example for us to follow.

The battle is always for our worship. We either worship God or the devil. There is no in-between.

The devil was no match. He had to flee when Jesus declared a stronger word than his.

It was from this moment in the wilderness that Jesus went out in power and began his ministry, performing signs and miracles to confirm himself as God and to seek and save those who were lost. Authority by Jesus was claimed, and power was then given to fulfill his mission. Jesus displayed a spirit that contained self-control, and therefore, dominion over Satan.

We can call on our Father through the name of Jesus. Believe that God has given you power, love, and self-control — a discipline to think with the mind of Christ. The Spirit of God is victorious over our battles if we submit to God's Spirit and not to the spirit of fear. When we feel like we are in the wilderness, alone in our battles, weary and beaten down by accusations and temptations of the enemy, we must remember his word. For in his word is active life and the power to overcome.

For the word of God is living and active, sharper than any two-

edged sword, piercing to the division of soul and of spirit, of joints and of marrow, and discerning the thoughts and intentions of the heart. (Hebrews 4:12)

We read it, yet the word of God reads us intimately. And the devil knows its power when someone believes. Notice Jesus was fasting for 40 days at this time. His ability to act in authority came from a place of intimacy. Intimacy produces authority, which is why it is integral to know God's nature. Jesus' mind was clear on the Father's words — not distracted by the temptations of this world or his flesh — because he was communing in his Father's presence.

AUTHORITY OVER THOUGHTS AND STRONGHOLDS OF THE MIND

Our authority in Christ is developed when we abide in his word. When his word is incubated in the depths of our heart, faith can be birthed. Hide his word in your heart and treasure it. Spend time remembering his word. We must meditate on his thoughts for us and not our own opinions. This is what it is to have the mind of Christ. We can think like Christ when we abide in him.

"For who has understood the mind of the Lord so as to instruct him?" But we have the mind of Christ. (1 Corinthians 2:16)

There is another way in which our authority grows, and that is through experiencing trial and temptation. When we lean on Christ and overcome during times of trial and temptation, there is an authority over the weapons formed against us. We can say in Christ that nothing of this world has a hold on us. We have received power and an ability to defy accusations, temptations, and potentially destroying circumstances. This type of living confuses the devil. His power is nullified when the pressing of his plans are not submitted to.

Walking in the pathway of God's presence requires you to follow Jesus. Jesus destroyed the works of the enemy, and so do we — in his power. Jesus came to seek and save that which was lost, and so do we — in his saving power.

Listen to the strong language used by the Apostle Paul regarding counteracting words of the enemy that come through mankind.

For though we walk in the flesh, we are not waging war according to the flesh. For the weapons of our warfare are not of the flesh but have divine power to destroy strongholds. We destroy arguments and every lofty opinion raised against the knowledge of God, and take every thought captive to obey Christ, being ready to punish every disobedience, when your obedience is complete. (2 Corinthians 10:3–6)

To love God with your mind is to continue to disallow any lofty concept or false ideal to exalt itself above him in your thinking.

Strongholds are fortified castles around our mind and thoughts. They attempt to keep us bound and trapped. We are not called to demolish each other with our arguments but to demolish the devil's strongholds. In the context of this passage, Paul was facing pagan philosophical arguments from others that tried to minimize the Gospel. The same also can be applied for us as individuals. There is divine power to destroy every lofty thought that says otherwise about who God is, the image we are made in, and the mission of our life.

The knowledge of God is not just speaking of an intellectual understanding but an intimate experiential knowing. Even Satan knows the word of God. Anyone can quote it, yet our charge is to know Jesus who embodies the word and also the words Jesus tells us. The book of Ephesians tells us that God desires for us to have his wisdom and knowledge (Ephesians 1:16-17). This is not some lofty, hidden secret to life that we cannot attain. It is an invitation to deep, personal obedience. To be wise is to obey God — to know him intimately. To be foolish is to ignore him. Jesus, who is true wisdom and knowledge, has now been made known and accessible to us all by the Spirit of God.

We must learn not to tolerate Satan's lies like Elijah did. We don't argue with demonic forces. We can simply declare the promises and power of the word through prayer when any accusation or argument comes in an attempt to raise itself above God's word. This is what Jesus did! In doing so, we show Satan's accusations to hold no weight. Through Jesus, we have pulled apart any argument or deception or claim that we are guilty, shameful, or intimidated by fear. Every time an irrational thought that is contrary to God's nature enters our mind, we can destroy it by holding it up against the light of God's word. This is one major way we can love God with all of our minds.

Much of 2 Corinthians 10 speaks in military and war language. Captives were often taken to the General of the army and paraded through the streets as a trophy of victory. We do the same with our thoughts. We practice taking them captive by the help of the Holy Spirit, and we bring them to submit to the truth of Jesus the King who has all victory and authority.

> *We are people of his presence, and therefore, his word. We are not called to entertain speculation — what may happen — we are called to walk in revelation — what has happened in Jesus Christ.*

AUTHORITY IN WORSHIP

Learning to use weapons that are not of the flesh takes practice through abiding in the Holy Spirit's presence and knowing the word. The path of his presence requires you to be equipped with many offensive weapons through Christ to live as overcomers. One of those weapons is worship.

Worship is not only glorifying God, it is also a weapon of authority in our life. Worship requires faith, and God responds to it. There is a preserving quality about worshiping God that keeps us from self-destructing as "lords" of our own life.

We have learnt already that, as disciples, we are all priests unto God, ministering and offering him the worship of our lives as an example to the world.

It was common for the tribe of Levite priests to be on the frontline of battle in worship. In the Old Testament, Judah was under siege from Edom. Israel's King Jehoshaphat instructed the Levite priests to go out before the army and worship. Look what happened:

And when he had taken counsel with the people, he appointed those who were to sing to the LORD and praise him in holy attire, as they went before the army, and say,

"Give thanks to the LORD,
for his steadfast love endures forever."

And when they began to sing and praise, the LORD set an ambush against the men of Ammon, Moab, and Mount Seir, who had come against Judah, so that they were routed. For the men of Ammon and Moab rose against the inhabitants of Mount Seir, devoting them to destruction, and when they had made an end of the inhabitants of Seir, they all helped to destroy one another. (2 Chronicles 20:21–23)

When the priests gave thanks to God and sang of his love, the Lord threw the opposing armies into chaos, and they destroyed themselves. This story is a powerful description of what takes place in the spirit realm when we worship. It makes no sense to Satan when we offer up praise and worship in the midst of fear and times of hardship. It sends his plans and accusations into chaos. Satan's power is useless as we thank God for the battle that he fights for us. We see that Judah did not have to fight physically, but worshiped instead.

And he said, "Listen, all Judah and inhabitants of Jerusalem and King Jehoshaphat: Thus says the LORD to you, 'Do not be afraid and do not be dismayed at this great horde, for the battle is not yours but God's.

You will not need to fight in this battle. Stand firm, hold your position, and see the salvation of the LORD on your behalf, O Judah and Jerusalem.' Do not be afraid and do not be dismayed. Tomorrow go out against them, and the LORD will be with you." (2 Chronicles 20:15, 17)

Worship may feel like the last thing you wish to do, or even a foolish thing to do, but it is the path to walking in God's authority. Victory, like Moses knew, was found in the presence of God, for the Lord was with them.

When we worship, we host an atmosphere of faith and his presence that invites Jesus to act on our behalf.

Heaven can invade our circumstances when we wage war through worship. The battle really does belong to God. Our role is to lift up the name of Jesus. When we make a stand, worship, pray, seek his face, and act in faith, his presence overcomes.

On the Mount of Temptation, Jesus did not back away. His actions were offensive to Satan. There is great power in God's authority, God has equipped us to live this life on the offense, not just defending and surviving. Next we will see that the Bible describes the armor of God that we are to put on in order to press forward and persevere in times of evil.

AUTHORITY WITH THE ARMOR OF GOD

Therefore take up the whole armor of God, that you may be able to withstand in the evil day, and having done all, to stand firm. Stand therefore, having fastened on the belt of truth, and having put on the breastplate of righteousness, and, as shoes for your feet, having put on the readiness given by the gospel of peace. In all circumstances take up the shield of faith, with which you can extinguish all the flaming darts of the evil one; and take the helmet of salvation, and the sword of the Spirit, which is the word of

God, praying at all times in the Spirit, with all prayer and supplication. To that end, keep alert with all perseverance, making supplication for all the saints. (Ephesians 6:13–18)

Paul wrote about several items of armor as it relates to the attributes of God. Often, they are prescribed to the armor of a Roman soldier, given the times in which Paul lived. Although he was often surrounded by their intimidating apparel, Paul is not describing the strength of Roman armor. The Romans and their beliefs were the antithesis to the Kingdom of God. We have already seen that the fight does not warrant worldly weapons. Paul is a Jew and a Roman citizen. He is well versed on history and grounded in Old Testament writings. He is describing the armor of God as divine. The imagery he tells of depicts God as a redeemer warrior.

The image of the divine warrior with his enemies is portrayed in the Old Testament.

> *He saw that there was no man,*
>   *and wondered that there was no one to intercede;*
> *then his own arm brought him salvation,*
>   *and his righteousness upheld him.*
> *He put on righteousness as a breastplate,*
>   *and a helmet of salvation on his head;*
> *he put on garments of vengeance for clothing,*
>   *and wrapped himself in zeal as a cloak. (Isaiah 59:16–17)*

In this context, Israel had made itself an enemy against God. The righteousness and just living were far off, and it displeased the Lord. God would be the warrior they would encounter, bringing judgment for the transgressor and salvation for those who fear him.

Proverbs 30:5 says, "[God] is a shield to those who take refuge in him."

The armor of God would ultimately point to the prophecies of Jesus the Messiah. The coming King would wear righteousness as a belt around his waist and faithfulness as a belt around his loins. In his second coming, Jesus will return as a warrior riding out on a white horse with a sharp sword coming from his mouth with which to judge all nations **(Revelation 19:11–16)**.

Jesus too would be the good news that we get to share!

> *How beautiful upon the mountains*
>   *are the feet of him who brings good news,*
> *who publishes peace, who brings good news of happiness,*
>   *who publishes salvation,*
> *ho says to Zion, "Your God reigns." (Isaiah 52:7)*

The focus of Ephesians 6 is different to the passages in Isaiah. In the Old Testament, God is the warrior wielding his powerful and holy attributes towards humans. In the New Testament, the transfer of the divine armor is now upon humans as warriors who fight cosmic powers of darkness in the spirit realm. The script is now upon us as disciples of Christ to be clothed in power for good works.

We don't wear Roman armor, but figuratively, priestly attire. We participate in the cosmic activity of God by engaging in worship, ministering the word of God in faith and in the peace and truth of Jesus Christ.

The whole emphasis of Ephesian 6 is to guard what is holy in times of evil. As discussed, this is what the priestly role was — to protect what was uncommon and holy against profane and common actions at all costs. Why? Because as hosts of his holy presence, there is great blessing for all.

It is an amazing thought that we get to wear God's armor — clothed in Jesus. Walking in God's armor is simply being continuously conscious of the person of Christ. We appropriate his attributes, symbolized by pieces of armor, that empower us as we are led by the Holy Spirit to action. As we "pray at all times" we are reminding ourselves and the spiritual forces at hand that God's strength and might is greater.

Remember, it's his armor and his battle. Our job is to stand clothed in him! Learn what it is to walk as a priest in peace, righteousness, faith, truth, salvation, and his word through the empowering Holy Spirit.

The enemy would love for you to just get by and to lull you into simply coping in your walk with God. The motive of his warfare may not cause you to walk away from God, but he aims to discourage you so that you no longer believe in God's power to deliver you from your circumstances. Be alert!

AUTHORITY TO WITNESS

Before Jesus ascended to Heaven to leave this Earth, he charged his disciples to wait in Jerusalem to receive a promise from the Father (see Acts 1:4). The promise was that they would be baptized, not with water, but with the Holy Spirit. There is a gift for us as followers of Christ, and it is the infilling or being immersed with the

Holy Spirit.

But you will receive power when the Holy Spirit has come upon you, and you will be my witnesses in Jerusalem and in all Judea and Samaria, and to the end of the earth. (Acts 1:8)

The word for "power" in Greek is *dunamis*. It's where we get our English word, "dynamite." It encompasses an ability, a might, a strength, a moral power, and a power to do miracles. Waiting fervently upon the Lord enables us to receive from him. The disciples weren't even sure what they were waiting for or what this promise would entail, but it was necessary for the path they would follow. The story tells us that Christians need the power of the Holy Spirit. Jesus was tempted with power on the mountain, yet power would come through obedience to the Father, not through Satan's offerings. His power and authority is a promise for all who see him and desire the Holy Spirit. The disciples had believed in Christ now that he had resurrected, breathed on them, and said, "Receive the Holy Spirit" (John 20:22). This was symbolic of what happened when God breathed into Adam in the Garden. The disciple's journey exemplified how they had become born again — a new man with the indwelling of his Spirit — by the breath of Jesus. When we come to receive Jesus as Savior and Lord, our salvation is secured (Romans 10:9) and we become new with his Spirit in us. It's impossible to know Jesus without the Holy Spirit drawing us and renewing us (Romans 8:9).

What is taking place in Jerusalem is another promise of the same Spirit. This is not just an indwelling experience, but rather, a baptizing in the Holy Spirit — an infilling experience required for the mission ahead of them.

While waiting in Jerusalem, they heard the sound of a mighty rushing wind — symbolic of the *pneuma* or Spirit of God.

When the day of Pentecost arrived, they were all together in one place. And suddenly there came from heaven a sound like a mighty rushing wind, and it filled the entire house where they were sitting. And divided tongues as of fire appeared to them and rested on each one of them. And they were all filled with the Holy Spirit and began to speak in other tongues as the Spirit gave them utterance. (Acts 2:1–4)

Everyone was filled, fire appeared, and there were tongues of languages. It was quite the scene. God's presence had come to manifest and make known to everyone that he is a consuming fire — as was in the case with Elijah and Moses. When the worship of "man" had occurred centuries before in Babel (Genesis 11), God dispersed the people and confused their language. Here, in Jerusalem, they were united, and God gave them a language that even other natives of that region could understand. There is a larger narrative at play than just speaking in tongues. The outpouring of the Spirit of God would signify the nature of the Spirit's refining work in the Earth, as opposed to "man's works" in the Old Testament Babel narrative. Power was given to God's people to serve his purposes. It's important to remember the baptism of the Spirit was given for us to be witnesses of Jesus. That's why we need to be baptized — it takes his power to see a soul saved, set free, healed, and delivered.

The promise of the Father is the power to witness Jesus.

The promise was fulfilled with the Spirit filling Jesus' followers.

The Holy Spirit is the focus of the gift and our intimacy. Everything else is a benefit! Without going into an extensive exploration of the baptism of the Holy Spirit, we find there is a distinct outpouring of the Holy Spirit up to five times in scripture. Three of those times are conclusive (Acts 2:1-11, Acts 10:44-48, Acts 19:5-6) regarding being filled with the spirit and the evidence of tongues as a separate experience that is unique from salvation.
The others occur in the immediate proximity (Acts 2, 4, 8, 10–11, 19).

You can and should expect to be baptized in the Spirit and also to speak in tongues. That is, to be filled with utterances not just of human understanding, but speaking mysteries unto God, that edify our spirit. Speaking in tongues as a form of prayer and overflow of the Holy Spirit in our life can cultivate a dwelling place of God's presence and awareness. It is an intimate place to hear the voice of the Holy Spirit for ourselves and others that allows us to live in a place of victory and empowerment.

If I speak in the tongues of men and of angels, but have not love, I am a noisy gong or a clanging cymbal. (1 Corinthians 13:1)

This verse implies that tongues may at times be human languages, yet at other times the tongues may not be human languages at all but rather may be angelic or heavenly languages. It may not always be the initial sign of being filled with the Spirit, but it can be a gift received in our walk with Jesus. The scriptures encourage us to be filled with the Spirit (Ephesians 5:18), not as a requirement to receive salvation but as an expectation for us to walk in the intimate and abiding power of God, and especially to be motivated by love.

AUTHORITY IN THE BAPTISM OF THE HOLY SPIRIT

Why is tongues an expression of being filled by the Holy Spirit? Speaking in tongues is a topic that has fueled much curiosity and debate. It can seem like a strange gift. But if God is Spirit, he is going to give of himself gifts of the Spirit. The Bible says when we speak in tongues or a language of the Spirit, we are uttering the mysteries of the Spirit of God (1 Corinthians 14:2). It is an intimate gift, and where there is intimacy, there can be authority. It has the power to develop communion with the Holy Spirit, to hear his voice and the instructions of Jesus. Who wouldn't want that?! The Apostle Paul talks about a particular use of the gift of tongues as a prayer language – as opposed to a human tongue or an understood language that was used to spread the Gospel experienced by the disciples at Jerusalem.

The New Testament distinguishes between a public gift of tongues not granted to all believers (1 Corinthians 12:10, 30) and the private benefit of speaking in tongues to God (1 Corinthians 14:2). The private use of tongues in our personal devotion to God enables us to be personally edified. It enables us to pray and worship according to the Spirit, and it can be used in our spiritual warfare (Jude 20; 1 Corinthians 14:14–18; Ephesians 6:18–20).

Peter was one of those disciples baptized at Pentecost. He was known for denying Christ and being fearful to accompany him to the cross. Yet in the succeeding chapters of Acts 4:1–4, he is preaching in the name of Jesus with boldness, and 5,000 people believed!

Peter operated in the anointing and power of the Holy Spirit after he got filled with the Spirit. Signs, wonders, and miracles followed his preaching and teaching — just as it did with other disciples after they were filled with the Holy Spirit. They were, as the word promised "witnesses of Christ," with incredible boldness, seeing wonders and miracles following the preaching of the word.

Boldness accompanies the authority of Christ. We may be timid in our own strength, but when we call upon the power of the Holy Spirit, we are captured by his perfect love and peace. There is no room for fear when our attention is solely on Jesus. When we know him we know his perfect love goes before us. You have been given a spirit of power!

For God gave us a spirit not of fear but of power and love and self-control. (2 Timothy 1:7)

Boldness is the after-effect of being baptized in the Holy Spirit.

Peter and John, soon after being baptized, were sent to Samaria to lay hands on those who had already received the word of Jesus and were water baptized.

Now when the apostles at Jerusalem heard that Samaria had received the word of God, they sent to them Peter and John, who came down and prayed for them that they might receive the Holy Spirit, for he had not yet fallen on any of them, but they had only been baptized in the name of the Lord Jesus. Then they laid their hands on them and they received the Holy Spirit. Now when Simon saw that the Spirit was given through the laying on of the apostles' hands, he offered them money, saying, "Give me this power also, so that anyone on whom I lay my hands may receive the Holy Spirit." (Acts 8:14–19)

If we read on, we observe a man that the people called "great," named Simon the magician, who saw the people being baptized in the Spirit and wanted to buy "its" power.

Give me this power also, so that anyone on whom I lay my hands may receive the Holy Spirit." But Peter said to him, "May your silver perish with you, because you thought you could obtain the gift of God with money!" (Acts 8:19–20)

There was an obvious demonstration of "power" that drew Simon to desire it for his own evil purposes. What did he observe? We don't know for sure, but it was most likely the speaking in tongues and the witness of miracles that followed. The path of God's presence invites you to come before him and seek the gift of the baptism of the Holy Spirit as a promise for you. Wait for him. It comes from dwelling in his presence, seeking him desperately through prayer and worship, and asking Jesus the Baptizer to fill you. Believe that you have received the gift of his power in faith and he will give you the "utterance" or "language." It will flow out of you like rivers of living water.

Jesus is the real, GREAT miracle-maker. He calls a withered limb to be stretched forth and be healed. He tells a little girl to arise from death, and she does. He calls a man dead for four days to come alive. Jesus even exercises supernatural authority over the elements calling the wind and waves to be still (Matthew 8:23; Mark 4:35; Luke 8:22). If that's hard to believe, Jesus encourages his disciples that they can do this too.

Behold, I have given you authority to tread on serpents and scorpions, and over all the power of the enemy, and nothing shall hurt you. (Luke 10:19)

Serpents and scorpions are animals that represent deception and death.You are called to have authority over these threats and realities.

And he called to him his twelve disciples and gave them authority over unclean spirits, to cast them out, and to heal every disease and every affliction. (Matthew 10:1)

Can you imagine Jesus turning and saying to you, "You have authority over all the power of the enemy!" Believe it! The invitation is still being sent out for those to believe in him and his words. You may start out with little faith, but you were designed to walk in the great power of Jesus.

SUMMARY

If you desire to be an effective witness for Jesus you will need his authority — the type of authority that sorcerers marvel at. It's the authority that forces of evil bow down to after their accusations and temptations have tried their best. Such was the case with Jesus and Elijah. Elijah called down fire from God with boldness and assurance in his name. He made a spectacle of the prophets of Baal and destroyed their works of evil. Elijah foreshadows the Spirit and power of Jesus, who ultimately made a spectacle of Satan and destroyed him once and for all. Jesus displayed the authority given to him by the Father on the Mount of Temptation. Using the word and worship of him would be the only solution to complete his mission to the cross — the place where authority over sin and death was culminated.

Jesus has given us weapons to walk in the path of authority that was given to him, and is now passed to us. They are weapons fit for a priest, which we are — having been made holy and able to walk with our conscience clean, for his power has forgiven us of sin. These weapons are not like those of the world. They are spiritual weapons of a priesthood for a spiritual fight, which is the place that our prayers and worship take aim.

Authority derives its strength from intimacy with Jesus, and intimacy leads to experiencing his love and power. When we dwell with the Holy Spirit, wait on his presence, and abide in his word, then we, too, are able to be effective witnesses of Jesus. Only then can we be equipped to go into all the world and preach the gospel.

RESPONSIBILITY

Mount Zion

To witness Jesus and his Good News of the Kingdom of God in a manner that glorifies him.

The final characteristic of someone who has been on the path of presence is responsibility. Responsibility can feel like a heavy, dutiful word, but on this journey it originates from a call, a beckoning, an internal compulsion to take up the collective charge of Jesus. What is this responsibility? Where was this point of encounter? How is this passed on to us, co-journeyers on the path of his presence?

It has always been God's design that we live with mission and purpose — or another way of saying this is with responsibility. Responsibility not only gives us an opportunity for partnership with God — which is a gift! — but God also wired us to benefit and thrive when we carry and dig into a given responsibility. We talk so much about us trusting God but God also entrusts us with great responsibility and invites us to be co-laborers in his grand plan for humanity and history. What an honor! In the Garden, humans served as caretakers and stewards of what God had given for them to enjoy. Adam was to "make" names for the animals and cultivate the Garden God gave. Later, the same principle applied to the priests in the Tabernacle and then the Temple. Israel was to "make" known the name of God through serving in the Tabernacle and keeping it holy, a type of spiritual cultivation. The Creation and Temple narratives' responsibility was to take the presence of God to the ends of the Earth.

This theme of given and gifted responsibility continuously shows up in the recorded Bible stories of people who walked with God. This is true in our own lives, too. Our stories only make sense as part of his story. And as we participate by owning and engaging in the responsibility of taking his story and name to the ends of the Earth, we experience the benefits of operating in our God-design as co-laborers, bringing the kingdom of God and Good News everywhere we go. As God's gardeners and priests, we cultivate places for his dwelling where people can be immersed in his presence and shown the revelation of God as they encounter Jesus. Through encountering Christ in us, others can be taught and baptized to follow the truth.

The first point of encounter in Eden gives us feet to stand on as we discover our irrefutable identity from the Father, full of mercy. In light of this, we then move forward in his presence and develop an attitude of humility through surrendered living. Next, our intimacy with him grows out of a conscious-covenant relationship, not obligatory robotics. Then, our authority in him is taken up as we own who we really are because of who he really is — all powerful. There are innumerable benefits of walking in the daily, consistent presence of God; and our character is continuously developed and changed and challenged when we spend time with God; but our final landing place in this book is with responsibility at a place of presence and encounter called Mount Zion.

MOUNT ZION

If you are familiar with the Biblical narrative, you might recognize this mountain from the final book of canon, Revelation, or from the Psalms where it's spoken of as a futuristic, mystical place. We'll get to these references later, but firstly, Mount Zion actually was another name for the city of Jerusalem in the Old Testament, a city built high on a hill and named by one of the greatest journeymen of the path of presence, King David.

Nevertheless, David took the stronghold of Zion – that is, the city of David...And David became greater and greater, for the LORD, the God of hosts, was with him. (2 Samuel 5:7, 10)

David's taking of Mount Zion and establishing this high place as a place of God's dwelling is so significant that sometimes his name is even used interchangeably with Zion. David and Mount Zion were inseparable in the biblical narrative. David represents a figure who was chosen according to God's heart (1 Samuel 13:14). David is chosen as a man after God's heart before he ever does anything and before he was even born. Therefore, the emphasis of "a man after God's own heart" reveals more about the revelatory nature of God and his choice, than it does about David's achievements or character. First, God's presence is worth everything. In his presence is blessing, and it is to be honored and kept at all costs. Second, God's presence is full of grace and mercy.

David exemplified what it looks like to carry the responsibility of spreading the story of the character and plan of our good Father — to spread the Good News of God and his reign throughout the land. No other king conquered more territory or lived at peace more than David. He would defeat Goliath and exile the Philistines and others from the land of Israel for many generations. He obtained rulership stretching from Egypt to Lebanon. What always remained with David — from a young shepherd boy to a warrior king — was the conviction that God fought his battles.

The key to David's greatness was that the presence of the Lord was with him.

He was adamant on bringing the Ark of the Covenant, a physical representation of the place of the dwelling presence of God, to Jerusalem. He understood that extreme blessing took place wherever the Ark was, and he was willing to gather 30,000 men to do it.

And they brought in the ark of the LORD and set it in its place, inside the tent that David had pitched for it. And David offered burnt offerings and peace offerings before the LORD. And when David had finished offering the burnt offerings and the peace offerings, he blessed the people in the name of the LORD of hosts and distributed among all the people, the whole multitude of Israel, both men and women, a cake of bread, a portion of meat, and a cake of raisins to each one. Then all the people departed, each to his house. (2 Samuel 6:17–19)

David was a king that served the people. In a sense, he had taken the presence of God dwelling in Eden and extended it outside the mountain of Zion to bless others. He established dominion, which was the original mandate for man in the Garden. David's story of encounter captures the responsibility we carry and are gifted with as we walk the path of presence, transformed and refined by God's presence. We are instructed around this responsibility before David — in Eden — but also after David — through The Great Commission. This call and spiritual assignment has always been God's plan to partner with us in the salvation of the world through Jesus Christ.

THE GREAT COMMISSION

Mount Zion was a continuation of the revelation of our invitation to take up the responsibility of bringing the knowledge of the power and presence of God out into the world. But there is another mountain in the New Testament where we (yes, you!) are read into the story.

Now the eleven disciples went to Galilee, to the mountain to which Jesus had directed them. And when they saw him they worshiped him, but some doubted. And Jesus came and said to them, "All authority in heaven and on earth has been given to me. Go therefore and make disciples of all nations, baptizing them in the name of the Father and of the Son and of the Holy Spirit, teaching them to observe all that I have commanded you. And behold, I am with you always, to the end of the age." (Matthew 28:16–20)

This is the responsibility we are given and gifted as participants on the path of presence. We know that our identity is as sons and daughters of the King. We take on the humility of knowing who and whose we are. We develop greater intimacy with God our Father the more time we spend in his presence. And we know the authority we live and — in this commissioning — "go" in. We clearly see what our role is — to make disciples and see them follow and obey the words of Christ, just as we have been made, and as we have followed and, as we have obeyed.

The commissioning is not just about the call. How does the delegation of responsibility end? "Behold, I am with you always." The presence! The indwelling presence of God is the impetus, the empowerment, and the strategy behind moving forward with the call, our God-given responsibility. Our "going" is not without him. We do not outgrow or attain perfection on the path of presence so that we go without him. The "with him" piece is the crux of the call. The commission is a co-mission — a mission that we accompany Jesus on and also the community of others.

The Great Commission was a reiteration of the original commission humanity was given at the beginning in the garden.

This responsibility we acquire on the path of presence may be straightforward in its call, but it is wide reaching in its application. To make disciples and live in a way that demonstrates the love and grace of God to those around us looks different, unique to us, on a daily basis. We are going to spend the remaining part of this chapter looking at a handful of ways our responsibility is carried by various personalized responsibilities in our life that actually hold great spiritual significance and are affected by time spent in the presence of God.

So where does this God-gifted responsibility show up in our various responsibilities and areas of life? Well, it begins to affect and be revealed in our work, in our character, in our remembering practices, in our gratitude, in our service, in our love, in our giftings, in our given anointing, and in our communal living as the Body and Bride of Christ.

IN OUR WORK

The first outworking of this responsibility found on the path of presence is in our work. Let's look at the very first occurrence of work in the Bible:

The LORD God took the man and put him in the garden of Eden to work it and keep it. (Genesis 2:15)

This might not seem that spectacular of a role, yet Adam being placed in the Garden has a prophetic aspect to it, and it's found in the use of the original Hebrew language. The words "work and keep" in the Hebrew Bible are *Abad* and *Shamar*. These are the same words used for the jobs of the Levitical priests to "serve/work" and "guard/keep" the house of God — the Tabernacle or the Temple.

And the LORD spoke to Moses, saying, "Bring the tribe of Levi near, and set them before Aaron the priest, that they may minister to him. They shall keep guard over him and over the whole congregation before the tent of meeting, as they minister at the tabernacle. They shall guard all the furnishings of the tent of meeting, and keep guard over the people of Israel as they minister at the tabernacle." (Numbers 3:5–8)

Working, keeping, serving, and guarding all were functions of Adam. Later on, they were functions of the priests of Israel. The instructions are to preserve what is holy from becoming profaned or unclean. By doing so, the people can be blessed because the presence of God can remain with them.

Thousands of years have passed since Adam and Eve were placed in the Garden. Today, our responsibility has not changed in terms of "keeping" God's commandments (the holy word of God) and his presence (ultimately given in Jesus) in our lives. We are also to "serve" the people around us, extending his goodness so that the world may know him.

IN OUR CHARACTER

The next area affected by our responsibility that is found in The Great Commission is our character. Whether you are a mom raising children or you work as a barista or businessman, your mission is to make disciples. Disciples are made not just by what we say, but by people seeing our lives and how we abide in Jesus and his words. In order to do that, it requires living in awareness of his presence, of the person of the Holy Spirit. Discipleship requires dwelling with Jesus just as the disciples of the Bible did. They were with Jesus 24 hours a day, gleaning and observing his character and ways. If they were going to replicate the purpose of Jesus on Earth, then they needed to be able to abide in the power that Jesus had given them in the Holy Spirit.

If we are to keep what is holy (his presence), then it requires that we walk in a manner worthy of what we have been given in Jesus. This can be, in part, defined as our character, as the Apostle Paul urges us in Ephesians 4:1–3:

I therefore, a prisoner for the Lord, urge you to walk in a manner worthy of the calling to which you have been called, with all humility and gentleness, with patience, bearing with one another in love, eager to maintain the unity of the Spirit in the bond of peace.

Did David walk worthy? As mentioned, King David was a king chosen after God's own heart. But what made God declare such a significant statement? After all, for all of David's triumphs and his courage in battle, there are also many failures and grievous sins. This was a person that committed adultery with a woman whose husband was at war. David then had her husband, Uriah, murdered. You could argue his sins were even more numerous than King Saul's before him. These moments hardly reflect a worthy "character" to be called a man after God's heart. If Jesus is sinless, David is sinful.

Yet God doesn't lie, so what is he getting at with David? Here it is: Every time David's character fails, he takes personal responsibility. His responsibility starts with acknowledging that he has sinned against God first and the people second. He also understands God's merciful nature. Here is one example, after confessing adultery and murder.

David said to Nathan, "I have sinned against the LORD." And Nathan said to David, "The LORD also has put away your sin; you shall not die." (2 Samuel 12:13)

David took responsibility for his own sin; Jesus took responsibility for all of our sins. David was a man after God's own heart because his heart knew how to repent and turn back to God.

David understood the key to life — that if he was to rule and reign as God wanted him to, then he would need the presence of God. And if his character failed and caused God's hand to be lifted from him, then his life was not worth living. David's first concern after he sinned was the grieving of God's heart. He was not concerned how he looked or how it affected his own kingdom. He showed humility, and that is why he was a man after God's heart. This attribute is what Christ is like. He would go on to write a Psalm after he had committed adultery with Bathsheba, Uriah's wife. Listen to David's cry for mercy — the same mercy described in Exodus 34 to Moses. In 12 verses, read the words of a man who took responsibility in the form of godly sorrow.

> *Have mercy on me, O God,*
>   *according to your steadfast love;*
> *according to your abundant mercy*
>   *blot out my transgressions.*
> *Wash me thoroughly from my iniquity,*
>   *and cleanse me from my sin!*
> *For I know my transgressions,*

> *and my sin is ever before me.*
> *Against you, you only, have I sinned*
>   *and done what is evil in your sight,*
> *so that you may be justified in your words*
>   *and blameless in your judgment.*
> *Behold, I was brought forth in iniquity,*
>   *and in sin did my mother conceive me.*
> *Behold, you delight in truth in the inward being,*
>   *and you teach me wisdom in the secret heart.*
>
> *Purge me with hyssop, and I shall be clean;*
>   *wash me, and I shall be whiter than snow.*
> *Let me hear joy and gladness;*
>   *let the bones that you have broken rejoice.*
> *Hide your face from my sins,*
>   *and blot out all my iniquities.*
> *Create in me a clean heart, O God,*
>   *and renew a right spirit within me.*
> *Cast me not away from your presence,*
>   *and take not your Holy Spirit from me.*
> *Restore to me the joy of your salvation,*
>   *and uphold me with a willing spirit. (Psalm 51:1–12)*

It was paramount for David to dwell with God in holiness, clean-hearted and with a pure conscience. That should be paramount for those of us who desire to be disciples of Jesus as well. The Holy Spirit may not be removed from those who believe, but he can be grieved, and we are useless without him. God cannot hear our prayers if our hearts are tainted by withholding sin. This is the beauty of the gift of repentance.

What is at stake is everything — our dwelling with God is affected. We have removed ourselves from being in his manifest presence when we fail to "keep" his words alive in our actions. We run and seclude ourselves like Adam and Eve. Not only is our intimacy with God affected, but the people around us are, too.

As Paul mentioned in Ephesians, walking worthy in a manner of your calling is imperative. In doing so, we maintain unity with each other. Don't believe the lie that your individual sin doesn't hurt anyone. We are one body. Metaphorically, if the foot hurts or is cut off, it has implications for the functioning of the whole body and how it walks. Paul reminds us that we are part of one another like a physical body (Romans 12:5).

When God invites us for the mission, his power and wisdom are available to us. Our character and approach to his presence will determine whether we can sustain our walk in him.

Our responsibility is to be sensitive to guard his holy presence, because God has an inheritance for us and for others.

Or do you not know that the unrighteous will not inherit the kingdom of God? Do not be deceived: neither the sexually immoral, nor idolaters, nor adulterers, nor men who practice homosexuality, nor thieves, nor the greedy, nor drunkards, nor revilers, nor swindlers will inherit the kingdom of God. And such were some of you. But you were washed, you were sanctified, you were justified in the name of the Lord Jesus Christ and by the Spirit of our God. (1 Corinthians 6:9–11)

It is clear that disciples practice being washed by the Spirit of God daily so that our lives do not make a practice of living outside his inheritance for us — who is Jesus.

IN OUR REMEMBRANCE

In order to fulfill our responsibility discovered along the pathway of discipleship, we participate in God-wired remembrance practices. Pauses. Reflections. Holy remembrance of who God is and what he has done on our behalf. This repositions us and guides us back to the true north in Jesus. We have a responsibility to remember the mercy of God and walk in it. Remembering is essentially what we are doing when we worship God. We are living from a place of thankfulness and grace when we remember his goodness.

Israel was called to remember the ways of God and celebrate God's mercy in the Passover feast in Jerusalem. Several times a year, they would ascend to Mount Zion to "keep" the Passover — the time Israel was delivered from the bondage of Pharaoh. God instructed them to place the blood of a spotless lamb on the doorposts so that their household would not die. Death passed over, and every firstborn child was preserved if their houses had blood marked on the doorposts. The significance foreshadowed Jesus Christ, who was the firstborn of all mankind, and the true, spotless Lamb of God who was slain for our salvation (1 Corinthians 5:7).

For the LORD will pass through to strike the Egyptians, and when he sees the blood on the lintel and on the two doorposts, the LORD will pass over the door and will not allow the destroyer to enter your houses to strike you. You shall observe this rite as a statute for you and for your sons forever. And when you come to the land that the LORD will give you, as he has promised, you shall keep this service. (Exodus 12:23–25)

The importance of remembrance is stated here, yet Israel would fail to "keep" this service when they did enter the Promised Land. They forgot or ignored their responsibility to teach the succeeding generations to obey all the commandments God had given.

Now, the New Covenant has been established in Jesus Christ. The Gospel reminds us again to remember the Lamb of God that was given to us when he ascended to Jerusalem to be beaten and die upon a cross. Luke says about Jesus:

And he took bread, and when he had given thanks, he broke it and gave it to them, saying, "This is my body, which is given for you. Do this in remembrance of me." And likewise the cup after they had eaten, saying, "This cup that is poured out for you is the new covenant in my blood." (Luke 22:19–20)

Remembering the body and blood of Jesus that saves us, just like God saved Israel, is our first priority to fulfilling the Great Commission. When we take communion — the elements of bread and wine — we are remembering the life that Christ gave for us, the power that his blood carries for the forgiveness of our sin, and the boldness for the mission to share the Gospel.

David was known for remembering the Lord and his mercy, as was Moses.

Let's look at the opposite of remembering. God takes whining — a by-product of forgetting his benefits, seriously. When addressing the impatient sin of the people who had whined and complained against the Lord's provision, Moses instructed the Israelites to behold, to look and remember.

And the people came to Moses and said, "We have sinned, for we have spoken against the LORD and against you. Pray to the LORD, that he take away the serpents from us." So Moses prayed for the people. And the LORD said to Moses, "Make a fiery serpent and set it on a pole, and everyone who is bitten, when he sees it, shall live." So Moses made a bronze serpent and set it on a pole. And if a serpent bit anyone, he would look at the bronze serpent and live. (Numbers 21:7-9)

What is going on here? Creating fiery snakes to put on a pole sounds like pagan worship, but it's far from it. The story was foreshadowing of Christ, who would take the place of sin represented in a serpent. God was ultimately saying that anyone who looks and beholds the Son of Man, who was lifted up and became a curse for us, will live.

Christ redeemed us from the curse of the law by becoming a curse for us—for it is written, "Cursed is everyone who is hanged on a tree" (Galatians 3:12-13)

Sin was meant to be seen in a manner that, when you looked at it, you realized the consequences of its curse. But as you behold Jesus in its place, you will find salvation and healing.

This is what we are doing when we eat of the bread and wine around the Lord's supper. Remembering, looking, and beholding Jesus and his word is the key to a discipleship of dwelling in his presence. If forgetting can lead to sin, remembering can help lead us to salvation.

IN OUR GRATITUDE

As we internalize the weight of the call and responsibility found on the path of presence, something begins to take place in our perspective. Thankfulness wells up on the inside of us and the lens with which we see the world becomes one of deep gratitude. As we have seen, God takes complaining and grumbling very seriously. When Jesus announced that he was the bread of life that came down from Heaven (John 6:35-41), it says that the "Jews grumbled about him." The passage wants the reader to remember that the same thing the Jews are doing in testing Jesus is the same thing the Israelites did with God and Moses in the wilderness. They complained and whined about the provision of God — the manna from Heaven — and they longed for the food of Egypt, believing God had brought them out only to see them killed by their enemies. They tested God ten times (Numbers 14:22), turning away, worshiping other gods, and rejecting Him:

And the LORD spoke to Moses and to Aaron, saying, "How long shall this wicked congregation grumble against me? I have heard the grumblings of the people of Israel, which they grumble against me. Say to them, 'As I live, declares the LORD, what you have said in my hearing I will do to you: your dead bodies shall fall in this wilderness, and of all your number, listed in the census from twenty years old and upward, who have grumbled against me, not one shall come into the land where I swore that I would make you dwell, except Caleb the son of Jephunneh and Joshua the son of Nun. But your little ones, who you said would become a prey, I will bring in, and they shall know the land that you have rejected." (Numbers 14:26–31)

Their complaining cost them entrance into the Promised Land. Ironically, the Hebrew word for grumblings is *lun* (loon), which means to dwell, abide, or lodge. If dwelling with the Holy Spirit means moving in obedience with his voice and commands, then grumbling means dwelling or abiding in our stubbornness. We are prone to stopping in a place or mindset that God never intended for us to stop. What could have taken them two weeks took them 40 years because of their grumbling and unbelief. The pillar of cloud and fire of his presence that were moving signposts to lead Israel through the wilderness became immovable because the people's hearts were ungrateful. Even if the lesson wasn't how fast you could get to the destination, it was definitely one of learning obedience.

God is patient, as we have read. His love and mercy longs for us to be grateful for what he has done for us. Yet, he cannot force anyone's heart. It's a sobering thought to realize how much we miss what God has for us because we complain about who we are or what we don't have in life.

Paul's words about doing everything without grumbling or complaining ring even louder. Why? Because we are not called to be stumbling blocks of unbelief but to be lights in the world leading people to Jesus, the dwelling place of all promises.

Do all things without grumbling or disputing, that you may be blameless and innocent, children of God without blemish in the midst of a crooked and twisted generation, among whom you shine as lights in the world, holding fast to the word of life, so that in the day of Christ I may be proud that I did not run in vain or labor in vain. (Philippians 2:14–16)

We have the privileged responsibility to enter the promises of God found in the body and blood of Jesus. A generation was lost in the wilderness. We must understand that our obedience is another generation's ability to follow. We can be thankful that Jesus never complained and grumbled against his assignment to go to the cross, sent by the Father. He never forfeited the promise that was ours. He abided in obedience.

If we are called to dwell and abide, as we will see next, it holds the power for the mission to see people come to know Christ, and is also the thing we will be doing for all of eternity.

IN OUR SERVICE

Just as Adam and Eve served and worked the Garden of creation to extend its beauty and function, and the priests served and worked in the temple, so are we to serve by bringing God's presence, his Spirit, to the world. Is this not the same call Jesus bestows on his followers as he ascends into heaven?

Jesus came to serve not be served (Matthew 20:28). Disciples do the same. We are not of this world. As we have read, our home is the New Heaven and Earth, yet we are in this world to reflect the light of Christ.

Jesus spoke in the famous Sermon on the Mount and said:

"You are the light of the world. A town built on a hill cannot be hidden. Neither do people light a lamp and put it under a bowl. Instead they put it on its stand, and it gives light to everyone in the house. In the same way, let your light shine before others, that they may see your good deeds and glorify your Father in heaven." (Matthew 5:14–16)

Intimacy leads to knowing our authority which always carries the responsibility to serve others.

People are designed to see and know the life of Christ, which is the light of all men (John 1). It is not our little light that shines but his great light. Through our good deeds (that are only possible by the Holy Spirit) and by living and sharing the Good News (the Gospel of salvation in Jesus), we make the light of the truth visible. Current unbelievers of Jesus will most often see him through you. God's method to bring all into the light of Jesus is through mankind. When they do, they will no longer remain spiritually blinded or in the dark (John 12:46).

Darkness is related to the place of eternity called hell and any person who does not dwell in the life-giving revelation of Jesus lives in a state of ignorance. The Bible says hell is the final destination of which angels and men who reject Jesus will end up (Matthew 25:41, 46), a place of outer darkness and pain (Matthew 25:30). It is the opposite of Heaven, the New Jerusalem. God's fire represents his judgment. Those who give their life over to sin will bring judgment upon themselves and subject their lives to the torment of hell's fire (Matthew 5:22). Often people reject the notion of hell — the place of separation from God. Yet why would someone want God in heaven if they are to ignore God on earth? It is each person's responsibility to choose.

One of the ways Satan loves to deceive us is to have us believe that we are "good people." Most people would answer "yes," if they were asked if they are a good person. The reality is, the Bible says that no one is good (Psalm 14:3, Mark 10:18). Only God is good.

We are capable of doing good things, yet we are inherently sinful people falling short of the glory of God (Romans 3:23). There isn't a particular number of good things you have to do in life that can save you from sin and death. This is the thinking of a religion of works and no one can take credit for that.

For by grace you have been saved through faith. And this is not your own doing; it is the gift of God, not a result of works, so that no one may boast. For we are his workmanship, created in Christ Jesus for good works, which God prepared beforehand, that we should walk in them. (Ephesians 2:8–10)

Left to ourselves, our hearts are inclined for evil, deceitful above all else (Jeremiah 17:9). We have an incurable depravity of sin. It is only when we confess that this is the current state of our hearts and lives, that we experience salvation and his goodness. We don't have to go around, picking out other's sin for people to be aware of their need for God. That's the Holy Spirit's role. He convicts the world of sin (John 16:8). Our role is to carry God's presence and light to people so that they can see Jesus. When people see the true Jesus, many will see the filth and wickedness of their sin and cry out for mercy.

When Jesus went to live in Capernaum by the sea of Galilee, Matthew's Gospel says that he came to a dark and evil region prophesied by Isaiah in the Old Testament:

> *"The people dwelling in darkness*
>   *have seen a great light,*
> *and for those dwelling in the region and shadow of death,*
>   *on them a light has dawned."*

From that time Jesus began to preach, saying, "Repent, for the kingdom of heaven is at hand." (Matthew 4:16–17)

It is clear there are two dwelling places, darkness and light and no in-between. If there is one thing Jesus could not stop talking about, it was the Kingdom of Light. It was the very first thing he preached about: The Kingdom of God, the rule and reign of Jesus Christ upon the Heavens and Earth. Jesus said to us, seek first his Kingdom and his righteousness (Matthew 6:33). It is much bigger than being saved or forgiven. That is how we enter the Kingdom when we repent. While our lives will always remain in a continuous place of repentance (turning to Christ), the objective was for us to see the Kingdom of God and Jesus as its King. The Kingdom of God is at hand. His presence has come in Jesus and is here now by his Spirit. Wherever his presence is and his redemption is experienced, we have witnessed the Kingdom of God.

Matthew 10:7 says: "As you go, proclaim this message: 'The kingdom of heaven has come near.'"

Just as God sent the Apostle Paul who was blinded by the light of Jesus, the one he was persecuting, He is sending you to go into all the world. Wherever you are placed, your calling as a believer is to reveal the presence of Jesus. "As you go," implies obedience.

The commands of Jesus were not designed just as good ideas but as imperatives.

"But rise and stand upon your feet, for I have appeared to you for this purpose, to appoint you as a servant and witness to the things in which you have seen me and to those in which I will appear to you, delivering you from your people and from the Gentiles — to

whom I am sending you to open their eyes, so that they may turn from darkness to light and from the power of Satan to God, that they may receive forgiveness of sins and a place among those who are sanctified by faith in me." (Acts 26:16–18)

What a responsibility we are privileged with, to be witnesses of people encountering the light of Jesus.

IN OUR LOVE

Jesus was continually challenging the disciples. This is what his presence does in our lives. His Spirit desires to keep the revelation alive so that we don't grow weary in doing good (Galatians 6:9). The disciples wanted to follow. Their spirits were willing, yet their flesh was weak (Matthew 26:41). Jesus doesn't condemn us when we falter or reject his promptings to shine his light. Only Satan does that. Jesus convicts us to stay awake to his promises and commission. He is gracious, just as he was to Peter who had previously denied him. When we are in love with him, we should want to share him and tell others of the love and truth they can experience. The acceptance and reverence with which we carry the call, the responsibility found on the path of presence, blooms into a love response.

Jesus came to Peter and said:

When they had finished breakfast, Jesus said to Simon Peter, "Simon, son of John, do you love me more than these?" He said to him, "Yes, Lord; you know that I love you." He said to him, "Feed my lambs." He said to him a second time, "Simon, son of John, do you love me?" He said to him, "Yes, Lord; you know that I love you." He said to him, "Tend my sheep." He said to him the third time, "Simon, son of John, do you love me?" Peter was grieved because he said to him the third time, "Do you love me?" and he said to him, "Lord, you know everything; you know that I love you." Jesus said to him, "Feed my sheep." (John 21:15–17)

For every time Peter denied being associated with Jesus, Christ would later ask him, "Do you love me?"

It was a gentle and truthful reminder of his grace and the implications of his love. We are all sheep who have gone astray. It is only right that we tell others of the path of Jesus. Jesus was exhorting Peter, that if the Gospel has been given to him, give it to somebody else! When we delight in obeying his commands, we show that we love Christ. It's impossible to say we love Jesus or believe in him and yet not follow him and love the things he loves.

To love Jesus is to love others. You cannot separate the two.

Now back to David, he was a shepherd before he was a king. He was well acquainted with sheep and their stubborn ways. Yet David displayed a vigilant and caring approach to everything under his guard.

If David was known for taking responsibility for his sin, then the second thing that made him a man after God's heart was his service to the people of Israel — especially the impoverished, including his enemies. God was showing something of himself, foreshadowed in David and revealed in Jesus Christ – the one who came to serve mankind and die for those who would also reject him. He instructed us to love our enemies and pray for those who persecute us (Matthew 5:44).

David displayed a deep care for sheep, which translated to great compassion and graciousness with people. David's conviction before the Lord was to honor those entrusted to him — even those who came before him who tried to kill him (King Saul). During David's most successful period of his life, he desired to show honor to Jonathan, the son of Saul and a loyal friend who died fighting with David. David showed the importance of remembering and asked how he could bless Jonathan's family. A crippled man by the name of Mephibosheth was found.

And Mephibosheth the son of Jonathan, son of Saul, came to David and fell on his face and paid homage. And David said, "Mephibosheth!" And he answered, "Behold, I am your servant." And David said to him, "Do not fear, for I will show you kindness for the sake of your father Jonathan, and I will restore to you all the land of Saul your father, and you shall eat at my table always." (2 Samuel 9:6–7)

Mephibosheth was lame in both feet because a nurse had dropped him. His name means "exterminator of the idol of shame." His life symbolizes the powerful grace and the redemption of God to remove our shame of sin. Mephibosheth was born into a royal family and was living in a place of shame as an outcast with a physical disability. Those who were disabled could not go to the temple to worship, they were considered unclean. King David showed compassion and kindness — the *hesed* mercy of God — when he brought Mephibosheth back into the palace of Jerusalem, gave him a seat at the king's own table, and gave him an inheritance! This unexpected act showed David's character towards the outcast and forgotten. Mephibosheth would experience physically what all of us have who have been crippled by shame and sin have experienced spiritually. We were cut off from the royal line of blessing, feeling the adversity and pain of spiritual impairment. Jesus Christ would be the greater David, extending his life for our sin, that we may be reconciled to royalty and seated with him at his heavenly table, seated in the New Mount Zion.

The power of kindness is birthed out of the power of remembering God's goodness, not necessarily other's actions toward us.

IN OUR GIFTINGS

God has given us spiritual gifts to build with. The Apostle Paul tells us to desperately pursue these gifts for the sake of building up one another. There is a list of gifts we can grow in and experience found in 1 Corinthians 12:4-10, Romans 12:6-8 and Ephesians 4:11. The gifts found in 1 Corinthians 12 can often be divided into three categories. First, the gifts of power are faith, healing, and miracles. Second, the gifts of revelation are wisdom, knowledge, and discernment of spirits. Third, the gifts of inspiration are tongues, interpretation, and prophecy. All of these are gifts of the Holy Spirit that we come to know through his word, seeking him prayer, and eagerly asking and desiring to be used for his glory.

"Follow the way of love and eagerly desire gifts of the Spirit, especially Prophecy." (1 Corinthians 14:1-2 NIV)

The Gifts of the Spirit can only truly operate in the Body of Christ. One can only know their gift in association with others. Paul says to especially desire the gift of prophecy. Why? In one sense because prophecy speaks of who we are and where we're headed. It has the ability to remind us of the faithfulness of God as a Church, and at the same time, it encourages us to do good works. It's our responsibility to seek out the community that Christ has for us to reflect his glory while using the gifts he gives us.

Isolation is common in our world but foreign in the Kingdom of God, because we are members of one another.

IN OUR ANOINTING

As we continue on the path, now that we have been invited into the responsibility of bringing others along with us, the anointing that rests on us because of the grace of God and empowerment of the Holy Spirit becomes absolutely necessary to not only be aware of, but cooperate with. Jesus said this in the temple about his mission to serve others:

"The Spirit of the Lord is on me, because he has anointed me to proclaim good news to the poor. He has sent me to proclaim freedom for the prisoners and recovery of sight for the blind, to set the oppressed free." (Luke 4:18)

This is what David did when he served. This is what Christ did when he died for us. This passage was known as "The Year of the Lord's Favor," and Jesus was reading it out about himself, the Messiah. By the way, the "year" hasn't stopped, the time of favor is still upon us. The Great Commission requires that we take up the baton that was given to us by Jesus. Our mission is the same to proclaim the Good News, so that the oppressed may be free to see revelation of the light of Christ.

It's imperative that we are anointed with the power of the Holy Spirit when we proclaim the Good News, just like Jesus. Kings and priests were anointed with a flask of oil poured over their heads as a symbol of being recognized and prepared for service. We are royal priests who carry power for service and when we do, the order of God's Kingdom is witnessed.

The Spirit of God is looking for a dwelling place to come "upon" those who believe. Just as it was in the beginning, when the Holy Spirit hovered over the darkness and chaos, there was no fitting place to inhabit because there was not yet order. The Holy Spirit desires a place to rest. He created and furnished the land with order and beauty, filling it with all kinds of goodness, as the most inhabitable place for the creation of man (Genesis 1:26). Creation was proclaimed and man was made so that we could ultimately be filled with his Spirit, God's chosen place to reside.

Do you not know that you are God's temple and that God's Spirit dwells in you? (1 Corinthians 3:16)

The Tabernacle of Christ is within us to proclaim the Good News as Jesus did. When people see you, God's intention was that they see his Son in you by the dwelling of his Spirit.

A question was asked at the beginning of our journey. The question pertains to "What kind of dwelling are you building with your life?" Ask yourself in reflection of your life right now: Are people seeing Christ in you? Do your actions reflect the dwelling of his truth, holiness, joy, wisdom, love, and peace in your life? Do you treat your body as though it is a precious temple of his presence, not to be given to just anyone or anything? What does your temple look like? Lavish on the outside, a ruin on the inside? Is it clean and holy? Is it ordered with his priorities? Is it fragrant with his kind and merciful, forgiving presence? Is your temple a non-anxious presence in a world of chaos? Are signs and wonders following your life as you follow his word? Is it filled with his light and reflecting his glory and way, or is it full of the world and selfish desires? Ultimately, do people grow closer to Jesus when you are in their life? Hopefully you can answer honestly these questions as a devoted son and daughter of God in a manner that seeks to follow Jesus' example. If not, let the Holy Spirit graciously convict your heart to become a dwelling place of his presence and value wherever you go.

A responsible life says "yes" to living a life with Jesus as Lord.

We have come full circle. "Come, follow me," are the words we must be responsible for. Jesus will ask these words of us all. Many will reject him, forfeiting his very presence now and for eternity. But many will know the presence and conviction of love and assurance behind his invitation. His Spirit will lead his children who are spiritually orphaned to know the Father. In turn, God will turn the hearts of fathers to their children and the hearts of children to their fathers (Malachi 4:6). He does the saving, healing, drawing, and transforming. Our opportunity as disciples is to be part of the action to "witness" Jesus do his best work.

IN OUR COMMUNITY LIVING AS THE BODY AND BRIDE OF CHRIST

Growing mature in our discipleship means we are not alone but choose to place ourselves within the context of community, allowing us to learn from others. Independence is really a worldly term. We are called to be dependent on God and serve one another. This is true freedom. When God used individuals in the Bible for his purposes, it was always for the salvation of the nation of Israel. You can't simply be in a relationship with God and distant from others, even your enemies.

The New Testament Church applied all the things they had learned from being disciples of Jesus. They studied the word of God, prayed and had communion together. Their unity in Christ and selflessness with each other, and their resources, saw God's Spirit poured out in signs and wonders. As a result, many people came to know Jesus and became part of the Church.

And they devoted themselves to the apostles' teaching and the fellowship, to the breaking of bread and the prayers. And awe came upon every soul, and many wonders and signs were being done through the apostles. And all who believed were together and had all things in common. And they were selling their possessions and belongings and distributing the proceeds to all, as any had need. And day by day, attending the temple together and breaking bread in their homes, they received their food with glad and generous hearts, praising God and having favor with all the people. And the Lord added to their number day by day those who were being saved. (Acts 2:42–47)

When we are invited to life as devoted disciples, dwelling with God and each other, we can experience the awe and wonder of God, even in what first seems mundane.

God places us in earthly families (Psalm 68:6) and the family of God to submit and serve one another. A conviction to serve the body of Christ represents the characteristics of patience and endurance and long suffering that Jesus displayed. Satan will try to sell us the lie that we can do this walk by ourselves, but we must be vigilant to not let offense and disappointment derail us from the path of presence. To dismiss the dwelling together with each other is often a sign that our dwelling with God is distant. For when we are hearing his voice clearly, he will lead us to be reconciled with one another and to love his sheep, as he told Peter. God is seeking glory from us through the refinement process of discipleship. Immature actions will leave the root system of our lives shallow, continually removing ourselves from the very people who God has placed in our lives to help refine us. While God cannot tempt us, he can certainly test us, and he will use others to do so. A mature and responsible approach to the testing of our faith will see it as joy. This sort of joy can come only by dwelling with Jesus. It is supernatural.

Consider it pure joy, my brothers and sisters, whenever you face trials of many kinds because you know that the testing of your faith produces perseverance. Let perseverance finish its work so that you may be mature and complete, not lacking anything. (James 1:1-2 NIV)

Jesus exemplified this joy when he went to the cross and in how he loved his disciples to the very end. What a convincing definition of maturity! Another picture of this commitment is displayed in the language of marriage used in the Bible to illustrate the pursuit of the Bridegroom, Jesus Christ, to his bride, the Church. We have a responsibility to be the bride Christ is coming back for.

Ponder on this, Jesus is coming back for his Church — not a particular denomination but the gathering of the assembly of those who believe in him. In a typical Hebrew wedding, there was a betrothal period in which the bridegroom would pay a monetary value as a downpayment to her parents, then go away to prepare a place for his bride. He then would reunite to take her back to the place he had prepared. This is symbolic of the place where we will partake in the great marriage supper of the lamb because of the physical price Jesus paid for our re-dwelling with him.

Then I heard what seemed to be the voice of a great multitude, like the roar of many waters and like the sound of mighty peals of thunder, crying out,

> *"Hallelujah!*
> *For the Lord our God*
>   *the Almighty reigns.*
> *Let us rejoice and exult*
>   *and give him the glory,*
> *for the marriage of the Lamb has come,*
>   *and his Bride has made herself ready;*
> *it was granted her to clothe herself*
>   *with fine linen, bright and pure" —*
> *for the fine linen is the righteous deeds of the saints.*
> *(Revelation 19:6–8)*

Our role in the meantime, is to keep, guard, and serve. We preach

Jesus and his Kingdom and we co-labor in building up the Church so that we and the nations may dwell in the New Jerusalem forever. The Apostle Paul spoke of the significance of the Church.

So with yourselves, since you are eager for manifestations of the Spirit, strive to excel in building up the church.(1 Corinthians 14:12)

The Church is his body and bride, and we are called to live victoriously. Jesus said the gates of hell will not overcome it. In building terms, Christ is the rock (1 Corinthians 10:4), the chief cornerstone of his Church (Ephesians 3:20). This is why it cannot be overcome, because it is built on the revelation of the person and work of Jesus Christ. Satan's plans will be overwhelmed by every offensive effort of the Church. The defensive gates of hell will not be able to hold firm because of the work of Jesus Christ!

And I tell you, you are Peter, and on this rock I will build my church, and the gates of hell shall not prevail against it. I will give you the keys of the kingdom of heaven, and whatever you bind on earth shall be bound in heaven, and whatever you loose on earth shall be loosed in heaven." (Matthew 16:18–19)

To bind and loose is to prevent or permit. When the message of the Kingdom of God is declared and people believe, permission is given to access, when ignored they are forbidden to enter the Kingdom, the eternal dwelling place of God's goodness and reign. We have been given the Spirit of God that no spirit of evil should prevail in our path. If there is peace in Heaven, there is peace to be loosed on Earth. If there is joy in Heaven, the joy of the Lord can be experienced here on Earth. We must tell of the Kingdom of Heaven as Jesus preached.

Our responsibility is to obey the mission, to preach the Good News, and to strive to excel in building up the Church (1 Cor 14:12) — God's place of permanent dwelling. No matter what we do for a profession, we all are called to do this work.

God's heart for his people is that all should be brought into his Kingdom so that they may dwell with him, just as Mephibosheth was brought into David's kingdom.

THE NEW MOUNT ZION

Mount Zion in Jerusalem recenters the story on the gifted responsibility and invitation to live on co-mission with God all the way back in the Garden. We know we are included in this because of the mountain Jesus later stood on as he gave The Great Commission. This call — responsibility — invades every area of our life: our work, our character, our remembrance, our gratitude, our service, our love, our giftings, our anointing, our life in community as the Church. It would be easy to assume that this responsibility concludes as we enter the presence of God in heaven at the end of our life, but there is one more thing we need to know about the path of presence.

Every path has an end, a final destination. The path of presence is no different. As we journey in life we choose to live as disciples of Jesus, being continuously developed and renewed along the path because of the powerful, transformative presence of God. It's the effect of living in proximity to the presence of God. The path has a purpose: to rebirth us like Jesus so that when we reach the final destination — the full presence of God in Paradise — we enter as the new creation, through the initial work of salvation which was begun in us. What a journey! What a life we are invited into with Jesus on this path of identification and intimacy, as we walk in humility and authority simultaneously. The thing about the path and the destination is that they both include this responsibility we have been talking about. Our responsibility does not end with our entrance into Heaven. There is one more mountain we have yet to encounter: the new Mount Zion.

This second representation of Mount Zion is the New Jerusalem. While the Bible speaks of Zion as a place Israel worshiped God in Jerusalem, it also points to the eternal city of God as the dwelling place or Tabernacle of God. Read and listen to the revelation of the Apostle John.

Then I saw a new heaven and a new earth, for the first heaven and the first earth had passed away, and the sea was no more. And I saw the holy city, New Jerusalem, coming down out of heaven from God, prepared as a bride adorned for her husband. And I heard a loud voice from the throne saying, "Behold, the dwelling place of God is with man. He will dwell with them, and they will be his people, and God himself will be with them as their God. He will wipe away every tear from their eyes, and death shall be no more, neither shall there be mourning, nor crying, nor pain anymore, for the former things have passed away. (Revelation 21:1–4)

The New Heavens and Earth is not a secondary idea because of the fall. It is a return to Eden — but what Eden was intended to one day become. God's plan to extend the goodness and beauty of Eden to the outer parts of the world and nations will come to pass. In the beginning, there was no pain, no death, and no sin. So it will be in the New Heavens and Earth. Our eternal state will experience the greater beauty of what God has prepared for those who love and obey him.

Have you read where you will live forever? Here is a picture that describes what will be the place of God's dwelling with man. Interestingly, it is shaped like a much larger version of the Holy of Holies in the Tabernacle of Earth.

The angel who talked to me held in his hand a gold measuring stick to measure the city, its gates, and its wall. When he measured it, he found it was a square, as wide as it was long. In fact, its length and width and height were each 1,400 miles. Then he measured the walls and found them to be 216 feet thick (according to the human standard used by the angel).

The wall was made of jasper, and the city was pure gold, as clear as glass. The wall of the city was built on foundation stones inlaid with twelve precious stones: the first was jasper, the second sapphire, the third agate, the fourth emerald, the fifth onyx, the sixth carnelian, the seventh chrysolite, the eighth beryl, the ninth topaz, the tenth chrysoprase, the eleventh jacinth, the twelfth amethyst.

The twelve gates were made of pearls — each gate from a single pearl! And the main street was pure gold, as clear as glass.

I saw no temple in the city, for the Lord God Almighty and the Lamb are its temple. And the city has no need of sun or moon, for the glory of God illuminates the city, and the Lamb is its light. The nations will walk in its light, and the kings of the world will enter the city in all their glory. Its gates will never be closed at the end of day because there is no night there. And all the nations will bring their glory and honor into the city. Nothing evil will be allowed to enter, nor anyone who practices shameful idolatry and dishonesty — but only those whose names are written in the Lamb's Book of Life. (Revelation 21:15–27, NIV)

Our trajectory of discipleship meets here! The Great Commission spoken by Jesus, established in Eden, culminates in the nations walking in the glory of Jesus' light. The same precious stones and more that were located in Eden are present in the New Jerusalem — its glory is endless. Those who dwell there with God must be clean, uncommon to the profanity of the world. In order for that to be the case, we must pass through Jesus, who washes us, and we must be baptized into his death so that our names can be written in the Lamb's Book of Life.

The intimacy Moses experienced dwelling with God's glory on Mount Sinai, and David's encounters with the Spirit of God are incomparable to the glory of the New Jerusalem — our true home, where we will rule and reign, walking with Christ in the cool of the New Garden forever. This is the place all of our life points to and inwardly groans for. Paul reiterates:

For we know that if the tent that is our earthly home is destroyed, we have a building from God, a house not made with hands, eternal in the heavens. For in this tent we groan, longing to put on our heavenly dwelling, if indeed by putting it on we may not be found naked. For while we are still in this tent, we groan, being burdened — not that we would be unclothed, but that we would be further clothed, so that what is mortal may be swallowed up by life. He who has prepared us for this very thing is God, who has given us the Spirit as a guarantee. (2 Corinthians 5:1–5)

There's further clothing to be worn! A further destination of our true home. John goes on to describe the Church as an adorned bride. Our deeds are like pure linen, being prepared for the return of the Bridegroom, Jesus. The New Jerusalem reflects some of the Church's characteristics. The city is described as gloriously radiant, and the city is ultimately its people — holy and pure, wearing white garments, like a bride. This imagery may be hard for a man to envisage, but we all can understand the power of being free in purity. We keep and guard the Garden, and we serve and work in the world to bring the beauty of Christ's holiness to the wilderness.

And I saw the holy city, new Jerusalem, coming down out of heaven from God, prepared as a bride adorned for her husband. (Revelation 21:2)

Our resurrected bodies in Heaven (1 Corinthians 15:35–52), our future re-created glory is revealed in the New Jerusalem.

The New Jerusalem sounds amazing, doesn't it? But how do we participate in something futuristic? Is this mountain inaccessible to us until we enter eternity? We started this journey together committing to begin with the end in mind. The New Jerusalem is the end, yes? Yes, and you can start living according to the realities of this promised kingdom today. The honor and glory we are bestowed with in part now is sufficient for this temporary time on earth. Honor, power, and authority will see its fullest reflection in our exalted status in Heaven, yet Christ's fullness of his spirit has been given to us internally now. Before we enter this glory, there is much to do. It is important to realize that our ruling and reigning with Christ doesn't stop. The new Jerusalem doesn't have you collapsing on a couch when you arrive. No! God's creative plan for those who believe continues to be re-established, but this time not under the suppression of sin evil. The Kingdom of God truly reigns forever, so get acquainted with the King and his plan. By understanding the reigning that takes place in the New Jerusalem, we can start the mission to reign with Christ today. The end sheds light on our beginning.

There is no place for complacency along the path of his presence.

We have been given the light of the world. Our message and reality cannot be hidden or fall dormant because death and life are at stake. Christ is definitely not boring. He is the most radical man that ever lived. If we are not living alive in Christ, perhaps our revelation of his love and Kingdom needs a fresh awakening in us. We will find that we come alive when we have our purpose — our assumed responsibility — clear before us. Only then can we live in the present while participating in the future.

Responsibility to the mission has to be endued with God's presence — all efforts are in vain otherwise. In our doing, we cannot forget the goal and means of our existence. King David puts it best, summarizing the one thing he desired:

> *One thing have I asked of the LORD,*
> * that will I seek after:*
> *that I may dwell in the house of the LORD*
> * all the days of my life,*
> *to gaze upon the beauty of the LORD*
> * and to inquire in his temple.*
> *glory of the New Jerusalem, the Kingdom of Heaven. (Psalm 27:4)*

Presence: we know where the path concludes. We know the points of encounter and transformation on the path. This single minded cry of David's heart in Psalm 27 is the motivation. Yes, the reason we are on the path of his presence is for change, transformation, and for bringing souls along with us, but ultimately it is to dwell with our personal Lord and Savior Jesus Christ for all the days of our life, here and eternally.

SUMMARY

Dwelling with Jesus comes with responsibility. Responsibility to follow Jesus, to leave our selfish life behind, and represent God's character to a lost and dying world. We have a responsibility to tell of the Truth who is Jesus Christ, with boldness, and to display with faith, wisdom, and love the Good News of the Kingdom of God. All encompassed in his presence, with his presence, for his presence.

If David showed us anything, it was the trepidation he felt being separated from God's presence and co-equally the contrition he responded with in his repentance, always remembering of the good nature of his God. His story gives us hope that God's grace is sufficient in our weakness and all who call upon the name of the Lord can be saved.

We have the privilege of knowing God as our Father. We can experience the life and rest of Jesus when we live in humility before him. It is there that we find the intimacy of the Holy Spirit that we long for. He satiates our soul, filling us with power to walk in victory and peace. The way, the truth, and the life — found only in Jesus — has the authority we need to live as his sons and daughters and overcome the enemy — Satan. Jesus' authority is given as a responsibility to serve the world with mercy, love, and truth, leading the lost to Mount Zion, the New Jerusalem, the home of a true disciple. Its atmosphere is marked with the presence of Jesus as its light and life of the Holy City. For the earthly Mount Zion and the city that David built upon it, was a foreshadowing of the rule and reign we would have with Christ in the New Jerusalem forever. This is our real home, our eternal dwelling place.

Our trajectory on the path to being and making disciples must begin with his abiding presence and all that it entails. His presence is dynamically transforming, ever satisfying, quietly comforting, unceasingly convicting, and powerfully purifying. Learning how to dwell with him is the goal and means by which we can dwell and love one another. Our role as spiritual gardeners is to continue to extend the Garden of God into the wilderness of the world, showing those who are lost the way back home. We are overcomers, mountain dwelling people who bridge Heaven to Earth with a message of hope.

The vividness and reality of hell must grip our souls that we might "go" into the darkness with the boldness of light and extend the Good News to see those searching saved from its terrors of torment. If we are to be people after God's heart, we are to be people who love him with everything, withholding nothing, and loving others with the love that he gives.

So, in reflecting, does your life look like a dwelling place with Jesus? Hopefully by now you can sense the passion of Christ for you to continue the story of his glory and your privilege as a disciple of the King. Just as it was in the beginning, keeping, guarding, working, and serving in love are true functions of a disciple. They're hallmarks of sons and daughters of God. God is willing and desirous to walk with you as he did with Adam. What's more, Jesus, the second and greater Adam, says these words in Matthew's Gospel of chapter 28 that our hearts long to hear… "I'll never leave you," as you "go" in the path of his presence.

Go, make, teach, and baptize are the last of his instructions on Earth for us to obey. For dwelling with mankind is God's delight, beholding Jesus is our purpose, and his gentle voice invites you to come away with him.

And I heard a loud voice from the throne saying, "Behold, the dwelling place of God is with man. He will dwell with them, and they will be his people, and God himself will be with them as their God." (Revelation 21:3)